KU-075-861

Introduction: Money matters

Have you ever sat down and thought about how much money affects your life?

It's amazing to think of all the ways it can influence you, from your upbringing and education to your career and relationships. Money determines the social circles you mix in and the neighbourhood you live in. It colours your views on major issues like politics and religion. It even has a bearing on your diet, sex life, health and sleep patterns (especially if your finances keep you awake at night).

Indeed, analyse almost any conceivable decision in life – should I get married? Do I chase that career? Should I start brewing my own beer? – and money will be there in the mix. It's hard to admit it, but it's true.

Yet so many people clam up at the slightest mention of the dreaded 'm' word. We don't like thinking about it or discussing it. We would rather do anything than examine our spending habits or get to grips with saving. Some people wind up with debt, eviction and even bankruptcy rather than face up to their financial situation. For others, money becomes an unhealthy obsession – a constant source of stress and guilt that makes it impossible to enjoy life.

But we don't take action. We muddle through. We wait for another day to 'sort things out'. In the meantime, we find solace in tales of miserable millionaires and misspent lottery winnings. But we know, deep down, that things have got to change.

I'm going to help you to see that there IS a better way to manage your finances.

ALL I ASK IS THE CHANCE TO PROVE THAT MONEY CAN'T MAKE ME HAPPY.

– *Spike Milligan*

You'd be forgiven for envying people with rich families, well-paid jobs or lavish lifestyles. But it's another group of people who have got the real upper hand in life. They may not all seem wealthy, at least on the surface, but they are nonetheless part of a privileged elite – they are the ones who are happy with their finances, however much (or little) they've got.

These money mavens realise that cash is just a means to an end, a tool for getting on and getting by. They work for their money but they also make their money work for them. They manage to have enough money to lead the life *they* want, regardless of what they're earning. They save towards the future but they still find enough for little pleasures that they truly appreciate.

Money can be very effective – when handled carefully. It's like a power tool: great for putting up those shelves but deadly if you don't read the instruction manual! So think of this book as a user's guide for handling the money you've already got.

It won't help you to get rich quick. And, in fact, experts say that being 'rich' isn't essential for leading a fulfilling life: people do not necessarily achieve greater happiness once they have enough for the *things they genuinely want*. But experts also agree that we all need a certain amount of money in order to survive, let alone thrive. They argue over the exact numbers, of course. I say that it's down to YOU to decide. Once you've sussed out how much money *you really need* you'll be amazed at what you can do with it!

PART 1

HOW WE THINK ABOUT MONEY

Inertia

Inertia is defined by the *Oxford English Dictionary* as 'a tendency to do nothing or to remain unchanged'. For some, inertia seeps into every corner of life, but, for many, it is contained within a few 'blind spots'. So you might make active plans for your social life and holidays, but never really sort out your bank account or energy bills.

Why do you need to be on the ball when it comes to money? Here are some good reasons:

SAVINGS

A quarter of Brits have not saved money for a rainy day and a third rely on their credit cards for any emergencies, according to a recent survey by GoCompare.com. And, even when we do save, many of us miss out on extra money. The Financial Conduct Authority found that, in 2013 alone, £160 billion was kept in moribund fixed deposit accounts where interest rates (the extra amount you're given for depositing your money) had dropped below 0.5 per cent. The majority of those accounts contained balances of at least £5,000 – such big sums could be earning better interest in another savings account or placed in stocks and shares ...

INVESTMENTS

We may miss out on the opportunity to invest our money for a better return in the long run. A study by Barclays Bank found equities (that is shares in companies) outperformed deposit savings accounts 90 per cent of the time between 1899 and 2012, while £100 invested in UK equities at the end of 1945 would be worth £4,379 by 2012 – and only £185 if put in a deposit account.

BORROWING

A quarter of young people who don't get themselves on the electoral register are harming their chances of getting a credit card or even a mortgage in the future. When Brits do use credit cards, six out of ten do not pay off their balance each month, massively increasing the amount of money they will repay in the long term.

BANKING

Britain's banks sold around 45 million payment protection insurance (PPI) policies alongside mortgages, credit cards and loans between 1990 and 2010. But people paid for policies that they did not understand, had not asked for and – in many cases – could not use properly. Millions of people entered these agreements without reading the small print or questioning the bank salesmen.

PENSIONS

A 2015 survey from AXA Wealth found almost two-thirds of Brits are worried about not having enough money in retirement. Yet over a third had done nothing about the situation.

INERTIA ... IS HINDERING PEOPLE'S CHANCES OF SECURING A RETIREMENT INCOME SUITABLE TO MEET THEIR NEEDS.

- AXA Wealth

HOW GOVERNMENTS USE OUR LAZINESS

Governments across the Western world have tried to capitalise on our inertia to make us save for the future. In order to limit public spending on state pensions, policy makers are putting more responsibility on individuals to save into a pension at work.

In the UK, employers must put all their workers into a pension scheme as part of recently introduced legislation called '**automatic enrolment**'. Pension contributions are automatically taken out of workers' pay packets 'at source' (i.e. at the point when the salary is paid). So you are saving without even noticing. You can pull out whenever you like and get all your money back. But most are expected to stay in these schemes – all thanks to inertia.

Automatic enrolment is inspired by a new concept in behavioural science known as '**nudge theory**'. This argues that people can be subtly 'nudged' into positive behaviour that wouldn't come naturally to them otherwise.

Why do money matters end up on the back burner?

▸ *We crave certainty. Taking a decision which has an unpredictable outcome – often the case with money – is taking a leap into the unknown.*
▸ *We don't think we know enough to make the right decision – even though we have no intention of getting more information to help us out!*
▸ *Doing nothing means we feel less responsible for what may follow. It's better than beating ourselves up when we haven't got it quite right.*
▸ *We would rather avoid all the emotional baggage that comes with making a good or bad call.*
▸ *We think we're too busy to sit down and come up with a plan.*

We've all come across people at school, university or in our work environment who don't really bother. They turn up late, never hand work in and always miss deadlines. There could be many reasons for this, but psychologists now believe that some people may self-sabotage partly because they are overly concerned with how other people view them. So they would rather look lazy than incompetent. They sweat the small stuff and neglect the big tasks – like sorting out their money. No wonder so many people say they don't care about money management ... it's the perfect excuse for being bad at it!

Even the most successful investors in the world make mistakes. A 2015 article in *Fortune* magazine discussing Warren Buffett, one of the richest men in America, had the headline: 'My $100 billion dollar blunder'.

A survey by GoCompare.com in 2013 found that more than half of the population know they could manage their money better – but 15 per cent of those said they 'couldn't be bothered' to research the best options out there.

WHETHER YOU THINK YOU CAN, OR YOU THINK YOU CAN'T – YOU'RE RIGHT.

– Henry Ford

The struggle to delay gratification

The famous marshmallow experiment, conducted at Stanford University in the 1960s and followed up later on, revealed a startling fact: young children who resisted eating a marshmallow immediately in order to get two later on became healthier, wealthier and more functional in later life. Yet many people don't like waiting for rewards.

Why does this matter? Spending and borrowing less today allows us to have more money at our disposal, either to save for precious aspirations or insure against the worst. Yet that involves a sacrifice that can be hard to swallow. Of course, we all want to avoid painful trade-offs, but the problem is we can't really avoid them in our financial lives. It is tempting to live for today but we might regret it tomorrow.

For instance, if you want to go on holiday, and the cost is £1,000, how will you pay for it? Well, you might be lucky enough to be able to pay for it straightaway. Most of us would either have to cut back on other spending or use our savings. But those savings may have been earmarked for emergencies or other big purchases, so we would need to factor in that sacrifice too. Of course, we could start saving specifically for the holiday but that would mean waiting for it. Alternatively, we could borrow to fund it, but that's likely to be more expensive. That's because the cost of the interest on your debt would be higher than the interest you earn on your savings. Plus, repayments will eat into your income during the time you will pay it back.

WHEN MONEY
IS ONCE PARTED
WITH,

IT CAN NEVER
RETURN

- Jane Austen, Sense and Sensibility

Complexity

There is very little that is simple about money and how we use it. And that complexity can be a huge turn-off. To make things worse, the financial industry is often accused of making its products confusing and deliberately hard to understand.

As our financial options become more complicated, the quality of our decision-making can go downhill. We may choose a simpler route or do nothing at all, even when this isn't in our best interests.

Dr Ros Altmann, an expert in retirement finances, said in 2014: 'The complexity of pensions and the failure of providers to educate or help customers ... [have] prevented customers from making informed decisions.'

Infrequency

There are some financial decisions that we take every day, but others occur far less often. Ironically, the less frequent the decision, the more important it is likely to be. Here's how the decisions play out:

	FREQUENCY
Deciding what to spend or save:	**every day**
Assessing your budget and making adjustments:	**once a month**
Switching percentage of income into savings:	**once a month**
Opening or switching a savings account:	**every six months to five years (depending on nature of savings)**
Assessing investment portfolio:	**once a year**
Renewing an insurance policy:	**once a year**
Buying a home and taking out a mortgage:	**two to five times over a lifetime**
Buying a private pension:	**once in a lifetime**
Buying an annuity:	**once in a lifetime (typically at age 65)**

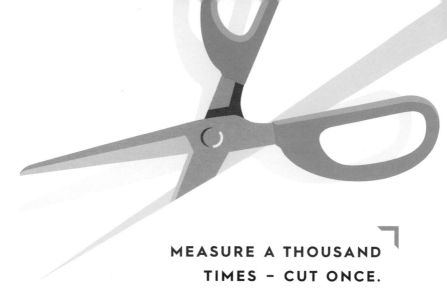

MEASURE A THOUSAND TIMES – CUT ONCE.

- Turkish proverb

Unexpected events

We don't generally prepare for the unexpected. So when our boiler breaks down or we lose our job, we may be in trouble because we don't have a back-up plan. Many people do not like dwelling on dark possibilities in life and tend to have an over-optimistic view of how things will turn out. The financial industry has long grappled with this problem and has struggled to convince many people that they would benefit not only from saving but also having insurance against losing their income.

So income protection insurance, for instance, is designed to replace your income when you are unable to work. But this has been a tough sell, even though it can be a salvation at a very difficult time.

Phil Jeynes from insurance firm PruProtect told an interviewer in 2012: 'With protection products you've got to put yourself in the worst-case scenario, and it's not much fun. People don't wake up in the morning and think "I've got to sort my protection cover out", because they're not very sexy products.'

The anchor effect

In a US study in 1999, people were asked a question about how old Mahatma Gandhi was when he died. They were either asked: 'Did he die before or after the age of nine?' or 'Did he die before or after the age of 140?' Even though both questions contained a ridiculous number, they influenced people's answers. Those who were asked the first question guessed on average that he was 50. The second group typically guessed he was 67. The great pacifist was actually 87, but the numbers suggested by the researchers affected people's guesses. This is known as the **anchor bias**.

People tend to follow the suggestions laid down by others, 'anchoring' their decisions to an existing benchmark. One group that has cottoned on to this is credit-card companies, who actually use a sneaky trick in order to activate our anchor bias. Once you know about it, you may be shocked at how much it can inflate your debt.

Most of us know how a credit card works – you apply for one and, if you're successful, you get a certain amount of credit that can be spent on a card but has to be repaid in the future. You can choose how much of the balance you wish to repay each month but there is always a legal minimum

repayment; failure to pay this leads to you defaulting on your debt. Any outstanding balance that hasn't been paid off results in charges.

Those who only make minimum repayments, which can be as low as 2 per cent of the balance, will take DECADES to clear the debt and could rack up thousands of pounds in interest charges. But a recent study conducted at Warwick University discovered a more disturbing fact: the mere presence on credit-card statements of a minimum repayment level leads people to pay LESS of their balance than they otherwise would. The anchor prompts people to make lower repayments and prolong their debt.

So say you have borrowed £2,500 on your card. Say the interest rate is 17 per cent and your statement gives a repayment level of 2 per cent or a minimum of £5 a month, whichever is greater. Here is what it would cost you:

You repay the minimum required every month ...	It takes 38.4 years to clear the debt ...	you're charged an extra £5,283
You repay £60 every month ...	It takes 5.3 years ...	you're charged £1,221
You repay £120 every month ...	It takes 2.1 years ...	you're charged £434
You repay £240 every month ...	It takes 1 year ...	you're charged £183
You repay £2,500 within 56 days ...		you're charged £0.

Being a hot head

Are you making decisions using the 'hot' or 'cool' part of your brain? The hot part of our brains (known as the limbic system) relates to our basic needs and primal urges. When this part of the brain is activated, we fire off intense emotions and feelings, even in response to rather trivial scenarios.

However, there is also a cool part of the brain, found in the prefrontal cortex, which allows us to make decisions rationally and calmly. When this part of the brain is activated, we can consider the repercussions of decisions, look at long-term considerations as well as immediate needs and analyse all the information available to consider the best course of action.

Now, it doesn't take a neuroscientist to figure out that we want the cool part of our brains to light up, not the hot part, when we're confronted with any critical decisions relating to our finances. The problem is that this reflective, complex corner of the mind is slow to wake up. Meanwhile, the intuitive part of the mind is quick off the blocks. That may be okay for more minor decisions – we can't agonise over everything – but it's problematic when dealing with the big stuff.

How do YOU view money?

You have probably formed a huge number of assumptions about money over the course of your life. Chances are, many of them are unhelpful. Tick the ones you relate to:

▸ *You're either good with money or you're not.* ☐
▸ *Money management is for total geeks.* ☐
▸ *Money is the root of all evil.* ☐
▸ *Personal finance issues are difficult to understand.* ☐
▸ *Caring about money makes people miserable.* ☐
▸ *Good financial management requires too much willpower.* ☐
▸ *You have to be good at mental arithmetic to manage your money.* ☐
▸ *It takes a huge amount of time and effort to get better at financial management.* ☐
▸ *Debt is inevitable these days.* ☐
▸ *The economic situation makes it difficult, if not impossible, for people to improve their financial outlook.* ☐

Some psychologists would refer to these statements as core beliefs. They are often learned in childhood and come to be accepted as cold, hard slabs of truth. We often don't realise that they are – in fact – as false as your great aunt's teeth.

But what if we flip the coin and consider some very different statements?

▸ *Anyone can be good with money – it isn't all down to personality, maths skills or earning power.*
▸ *Savvy financial behaviour can be learned.*
▸ *Feelings about money, either positive or negative, are determined by the individual.*

▶ *Money itself has no essential value except that which we place on it, and no purpose except that which we give it.*

▶ *Personal finance issues can be understood by those who engage with them.*

▶ *Being good with money requires no more willpower, time or effort than any other activity which you are highly motivated to carry out.*

▶ *People can achieve their personal financial goals with the right strategy, information, support and attitude.*

Not only are these statements positive and empowering, but they have the advantage of being true.

Money motivator

Write down five beliefs you hold about money and what it takes to be good with it. Be as honest as possible.

1 ....

2 ....

3 ....

4 ....

5 ....

Now think about your childhood. Write down five memories relating to money. Consider what your parents or guardians taught you about it (if anything). What was their financial behaviour like? Did they live within their means or live on the edge? How did that affect the way you were brought up? Were there any stand-out events – perhaps bankruptcy, divorce, a major windfall – that changed your financial situation? Finally, did you get pocket money or work to earn extra cash? Do you remember saving at all?

1 ....

2 ....

3 ....

4 ....

5 ....

Now find a couple of thoughtful allies to do you a favour. They can be sympathetic friends, relatives, mentors, your other half – anyone as long as you trust them. If possible, choose people who you think are responsible and 'good with money'. Show them your list of beliefs and ask if you can discuss it with them over a drink or coffee.

Ask them: what do they think of these beliefs? Do they think they are 100 per cent true? What evidence might there be to contradict them? Your confidants may want to swap notes and get your opinion on their beliefs. Do you notice any differences? What do you think has caused those differences? You may both want to discuss what happened in your upbringings and how it has moulded your financial outlooks today. Has it been for better or for worse? Each of you might want to get things off your chest. It might be very cathartic and even bring you closer together.

....

TIP ▶ *Only talk about this subject with your parents (or the people who brought you up) if you can all keep a cool head. If that's possible, it can be very helpful: they may offer information that was previously unknown to you, and that may help to explain what happened in your childhood. However, some of us have difficult relationships with our parents; sometimes, there is no relationship at all. These situations can arise through no fault of our own. What's important to realise is that we don't have to rewrite history or magically fix our family relations in order to improve our approach to money.*

PART 2

MONEY IN

PERSPECTIVE

IT IS NOT THE MAN WHO HAS TOO LITTLE, BUT THE MAN WHO CRAVES MORE, THAT IS POOR.

- Seneca

Could *you* live without money? Could you survive if you had no home, no possessions, only the clothes on your back? It's a sobering thought. Yet there are people living in your country – maybe even your neighbourhood – who face that stark reality right this second. Somehow, they find a way to live.

It's easy to forget that families all over the world struggle because they lack the basics we take for granted. Some don't have the essential resources of clean water, food and a roof over their heads. Others are locked out of education and the job market. The fact that many people still find meaning and joy in life, even when faced with abject poverty, should be a lesson to us all.

Volunteering

A great way to keep things in perspective is to volunteer at a homeless shelter, a soup kitchen or a food bank. Not only will you be helping other people, you'll be learning new skills, breaking out of your comfort zone and reflecting on what really matters in life.

Volunteering with a debt charity can also provide a reality check if you're living beyond your means. There are non-profit organisations that help thousands of people to get on top of their finances every day. They often rely on volunteers to fulfil all kinds of roles, from front-line counselling to IT support.

Stuart Carmichael, who runs a debt charity in Scotland called the Debt Support Trust, told me that volunteers are trained up to provide general information over the phone in just three weeks. Becoming a more hands-on debt adviser takes six months.

He explains: 'We start by giving them the overview to the charity and our principles. This is vital as many people don't realise just how life-changing asking for debt help can be. It's a frightening time where the average person has been dealing with debt for seven years before seeking help.'

Fitting this work into your life can help you to confront the damage caused by debt. We often ignore the long-term consequences of our overspending, but coming into contact with victims of our consumerist culture forces us to face facts. The experience allows us to effectively visualise what could happen tomorrow if we can't resist certain temptations today.

Websites such as Do-it.org can point you in the direction of local charities that need your time. Simply type your postcode into the search engine. You can also volunteer at community timebanks where everyone's skill is given the same value, and hours of work can be exchanged and traded.

Art and money

Art can also help us to get out of the materialistic bubble and into a new way of thinking. For example, anyone who reads *A Christmas Carol* by Charles Dickens – or watches one of the many versions made for TV and film – is struck by how happy the Cratchits are compared to miserable Ebenezer Scrooge. Life is tough for Bob Cratchit: he works for an abusive boss and earns a meagre income, so he can only afford a modest house for his wife and six children. His youngest son, Tiny Tim, is very ill and could well require expensive medical treatment. Yet we'd rather spend Christmas in this family's warm, loving home than round at Scrooge Towers – until the old man has his epiphany, of course.

Almost any great film, book or painting provides a different perspective on our money-driven world. Here are five favourites of mine. Why not make your own list?

1. *Silas Marner* – this 19th century classic novel by George Eliot follows the story of a linen weaver who loses his gold before a different kind of treasure enters his life.
2. *Into the Wild* – the true story of a young American who shuns mainstream society became a book as well as an unforgettable film by Sean Penn.

3. *The Great Gatsby* – the eponymous hero of this 1920s saga, penned by F. Scott Fitzgerald, shows us why money should never get mixed up with love!
4. *It's a Wonderful Life* by Frank Capra – need I say more?
5. **Almost anything** by Charles Dickens – he has a lot to say on money and morality.

The story of Aunt Mimi

Paul McCartney wrote 'Can't Buy Me Love' while the Beatles stayed at the five-star Hotel George V in Paris. An upright piano was apparently moved into the luxurious suite to allow the creative juices to flow. The song went on to become a chart-topping hit that cemented their status in pop's Hall of Fame. Later in life, McCartney candidly remarked that the lyrics should have been 'Money CAN buy me love', but perhaps he should have remembered the down-to-earth lady that raised his collaborator, John Lennon, in a humble house in Liverpool.

Mary Elizabeth Smith, otherwise known as Aunt Mimi, was adored by John Lennon, and he bought her an expensive house in one of Britain's most exclusive enclaves, the Sandbanks peninsula on the southern coast, after hitting the big time. A far cry from the modest Menlove Lane in Liverpool, Sandbanks seemed like paradise to John, who described it as the most beautiful place he had ever seen.

But Aunt Mimi's head was not easily turned. She revealed in a 1981 TV interview that John had stuffed her home in Sandbanks with presents, including the fancy pearl brooch she wore on screen.

With a raspy laugh, the 75 year old said: 'I could have had anything in the world. But I'm just one of those people who's rather spartan – and I don't want anything!'

Mimi did not have an easy life. She worked as a trainee nurse and private secretary. She lived through the Second World War, throwing wet blankets on incendiary bombs that landed in her garden. Later, her husband died of liver failure and her sister was run over and killed. John himself was gunned down in New York in 1980 – he was just 40 years old.

Mimi wasn't motivated by material gain. She had a bigger purpose in life that gave it meaning and direction – a life truly worth living. Clarifying what really matters to us is essential if we want to control our finances, rather than let our finances control us.

Money motivator

Here are three mental exercises to try. You can do these wherever you like – at home, on your lunch break, on the way to work, in a queue somewhere. Just so long as you close your eyes and concentrate for a few minutes. It might be a good idea to jot some of your ideas down.

MY SUITCASE

Imagine being offered the holiday of a lifetime on a tropical island – but there's a catch: you have to stay for three months and can only take the smallest of suitcases. What would you have to pack in order to survive? Could you live out of a small suitcase? What would you buy to put in there? Clean underwear, a good book, a special type of moisturiser? **What ten things would you need to keep your body and soul together?**

MY LIFEBELT

Say you lose your job or main source of income tomorrow. How much do you need to keep paying your bills for the next few months? How much do you have in your bank account? Do you have any savings? How long would that money last? Do you think your family or friends would help you? Would you look for another full-time job? If so, would it be the same kind of work? Or would you go for something different? Would you work part-time or set up a business? Perhaps you have to accept work that pays less than your previous job. **What's the lowest amount per month that you could be paid to cover the basics?**

MY TOUCHSTONES

Think of five things that mean a huge amount to you. It could be your other half, your pet, your favourite sports team, your looks, your home – anything. My list would be:

1. *Family and friends*
2. *Success in my career*
3. *Creativity*
4. *Me-time*
5. *Looking nice*

Now think of five activities that you most enjoy in any given week or month. My list would be:

1. *Hanging out with my flatmate (aka my brother)*
2. *Writing*
3. *Listening to and playing music*
4. *Going for a walk/run*
5. *Reading a great book*

Now take a step back and read through your conclusions to these three exercises. There may be some positive things to take away. Perhaps:

▶ You've realised that you could cope with whatever life throws at you. What a liberating thought!

▶ You take comfort from the fact that you don't really need that much to be truly happy in life – all you really need are certain 'lifesavers'.

▶ A lot of your possessions don't mean that much to you – you can manage perfectly well without them.

▶ The things that matter to you, the things you value, have little to do with money. Instead they are close relationships, a sense of community, a desire to learn and accomplishing things.

▶ You don't just do your job to pay the bills – it might be crucial to your identity and deeply held values. It matters far more to do the right job for *you* rather than earn lots of money.

▶ Losing your income would not be the end of the world – you've got a financial buffer in place.

▶ You have dreams and you want to make them happen. You might want a wonderful family life or to become a published author. You're in the driving seat of your life!

On the other hand, your answers may have shown you some uncomfortable truths. Maybe:

▶ You've spent a lot of money on things that aren't really that essential to you.

▶ You can't imagine living out of a suitcase. Your belongings make you who you are.

▶ Outward appearances matter a lot to you.

▶ You fear that friends and family wouldn't be there for you if you fell on hard times.

▶ You work hard on attaining a sense of status but you tend to neglect what really matters to you.

- ▶ You're not sure what you would do if you lost your job. You certainly wouldn't have enough money to survive in the beginning.
- ▶ You're only doing your job to pay for your lifestyle – it isn't really making you happy.
- ▶ You need a certain level of income to pay for expensive tastes.
- ▶ Spending and acquiring is at the core of your day-to-day life.
- ▶ Your daily life is not living up to your deepest values.

Your answers are probably a mixture of the good and not-so-good. Most of us are neither the Wolf of Wall Street nor Mother Teresa. If you're anything like me, you're just a normal person trying your best. But you want to live life to the full and you don't want to miss out. Above all, you crave respect and love from others. This is often at the root of our approach to money. We use it to feel 'acceptable' to our friends, lovers, parents, society – everyone.

For instance, I'd be lying if I said that exercise is purely for my health and enjoyment. Yes, I do it to stay fit, to get the endorphins racing around my body and to get the chance to listen to my favourite music through my earphones. But I also fear that I would be 'shunned' by others – particularly the opposite sex – if I put on weight. Even the songs I listen to, as I pound those pavements, often reinforce how much us humans 'need' each other, and how we can't live without love or sex!

WHAT FORCE
IS MORE POTENT
THAN LOVE?

- Igor Stravinsky

PART 3

THE
DESIRE
TO
ACQUIRE

PROMISE, LARGE PROMISE, IS THE SOUL OF AN ADVERTISEMENT.

- Samuel Johnson

The quick fix

What goes through your mind when you're tempted to buy something?

- ▸ 'It's a treat and I deserve it.'
- ▸ 'If it costs that much, it must be worth it.'
- ▸ 'What's the point in earning money if you can't enjoy it?'
- ▸ 'This takes my mind off my problems.'
- ▸ 'Having something new gives me a thrill.'
- ▸ 'It'll take me one step closer to being like the person advertising it.'
- ▸ 'This will sort out an issue that's making me unhappy.'

All those sentiments are entirely understandable. Buying something gives us a quick buzz. It's a very quick way to feel 'in control'. We're led to believe that we're rewarding ourselves for hard work, cheering ourselves up after a bad day or finding a guaranteed solution to a problem. I could be forgiven for thinking that a new shampoo, which is apparently formulated for dry and 'lifeless' hair, would be an easy way to transform my locks ... my confidence ... my appeal to the opposite sex ... my ability to win the love of a good man.

A good example of this for men is a perfume that was launched on the back of the James Bond juggernaut a few years ago. What man wouldn't want a little bit of '007' in his life? The sleek cars, the exotic destinations, the ridiculously gorgeous women; it's fiction, but so what?

Buying products gives us a shortcut to a better life – or so we think. We don't have to examine our behaviour, make difficult decisions or sacrifice anything except a few measly pounds. Heck, I wouldn't even have to get out of bed to buy that shampoo, thanks to online shopping. But the solution doesn't last long. If I'm not feeling secure or inherently 'lovable', no shampoo is going to change that. Unless I take proper steps to address my self-esteem issues, I'd become quickly dissatisfied and crave a quick fix once more. It's a vicious circle. And companies like it that way – otherwise we wouldn't keep buying their products and they'd go bust very quickly!

You probably don't realise this is going on. But almost every transaction, big and small, relies on this subtle process. If you're not careful, it can hijack your emotions – and ultimately your finances. So be aware of it.

YOUR INFLUENCERS

Next time you're browsing online, flicking the TV channels or even walking down your local high street, ask yourself: what do you really see? What's really going on?

For instance, think about the top five sources of information and news in your life. My list would be:

1. *Newspapers*
2. *Websites*
3. *Twitter*
4. *My friends*
5. *My parents*

Now, thinking back to yesterday, can you remember *all* the ideas that you were exposed to *just* from your top five sources? Probably not. We receive an overwhelming amount of information, and much of it can prompt us, if not actively encourage us, to spend money. The ideas we come across can play into feelings of insecurity and inadequacy, even if this is not obvious at the time. So, for instance, you may see an image of a beautiful sunset on a beach on social media and subconsciously think 'I want to see that in real life'. And companies, wherever possible, will try to co-opt that aspiration.

There is nothing wrong with aspiration. It helps us to achieve prosperous, comfortable and enjoyable lives. It motivates us to work hard, pursue long-term goals and innovate. It drives up our living standards, allows us to seek out new and exciting experiences and even gives us the means to care for and bond with other people.

But how do we know which aspirations are worthwhile in this age of information overload? In an ideal world, we would only spend money when we have identified a genuine need in our lives. But very often our spending can be a knee-jerk response to a narrative, image or idea planted in our minds.

What you see isn't always what you get. A print advert for mascara sold by Christian Dior and starring actress Natalie Portman was banned in the UK in 2012 after it was found that the Oscar winner's luscious lashes were mostly down to digital alterations in Photoshop. American beauty brand CoverGirl had to withdraw a mascara advert featuring musician Taylor Swift after similar complaints in 2011. And the footballer Wayne Rooney and pop star Justin Bieber were criticised after promoting sports brands and even flower delivery services to millions of followers on social media without making it clear they were paid to do so.

MANY A SMALL THING HAS BEEN MADE LARGE BY THE RIGHT KIND OF ADVERTISING.

- Mark Twain

The secret life of a journalist

I'll let you in on a secret. As a blogger and journalist, I have been offered a TON of freebies by companies. From expensive champagne to nights out at the theatre, the list of treats given to journalists – and put on the corporate credit card – is longer and more lavish than you can possibly imagine. But those firms don't offer something for nothing. Public relations officers take you out for the evening and pretend to be your best friend so you'll feel favourably towards them and the firm they represent. After all, people in the public eye can influence thousands, even millions of others with their words and actions.

THERE'S NO SUCH THING
AS A FREE LUNCH.

– Milton Friedman

Here are some facts to bear in mind as you navigate our complex consumer economy:

(1) Businesses provide products and services in exchange for our hard-earned cash.

(2) They have to gain positive promotion, compare favourably to the competition and generally make us feel good about the possibility of spending money with them, especially if their products are not essential to our survival or self-fulfilment.

(3) They never draw attention to the downsides of their proposition or the availability of better options elsewhere.

(4) They don't necessarily care whether you get REAL value for money once you've coughed up the cash.

(5) Firms are collecting as much data as they can so they can speak to your innermost desires. To them, you're not an individual. You belong in a pigeonhole. You're part of a neat and tidy demographic – single woman, student, commuter, hipster, parent – that can be tapped for cash.

(6) Media outlets earn money by offering advertising for business promotion. Newspapers, magazines, websites and blogs all need content, and firms spend vast amounts on having a decent share of it.

(7) Promotion is everywhere and it ranges from the obvious to the imperceptible. There are reviews, features, interviews and many other forms of content that exist purely to promote a brand.

(8) The famous and powerful are showered with free clothes, make-up, holidays, meals and gadgets – all in the hope that YOU will get to find out about them.

Higher cost = higher quality?

When it comes to painkillers, have you ever wondered why those well-known brands cost way more than generic pills? Both types of product contain the same active ingredients, meaning one works just like the other. Yet research by Which?, the British consumer organisation, found that big-name painkillers can cost eleven times more than non-branded tablets produced for superstores and pharmacies.

A paper produced by the University of Chicago Booth School of Business found that US consumers would save $44 billion a year by switching from national brands to store brands. The paper found that professionals like chefs and pharmacists were more likely to buy store brands, knowing that paying extra for fancier packaging and extravagant claims is a false economy.

In blind tests, shoppers often prefer cheaper versions of products. Whether it's lipstick or lamb, price is not always a predictor of quality – far from it.

IT COSTS A LOT OF MONEY TO LOOK THIS CHEAP

- Dolly Parton

False luxuries

Even the seemingly innocent world of baby attire can't escape consumer misjudgement. A 2012 survey by British shopping centre Lakeside found that a third of mothers can spend more than £100 on a single item of clothing for their precious offspring, and 46 per cent feel 'guilty' about buying any clothes for themselves.

What is to blame for this phenomenon? Perhaps we can look no further than celebrity parents, so often guilty of turning their offspring into elaborate fashion accessories. Luxury labels, perfectly coiffed hair ... these youngsters look like mini versions of the superstars that bore them. So we may feel that our children deserve the same kind of treatment if we are to show our true 'love' for them. But this is the very definition of a **false luxury**. There are no real upsides to spending more than necessary on baby clothes. Your infant will grow out of clothes within weeks or months and couldn't care less about what they're wearing. As for those parents at the school gates – they're too wrapped up in their own bundle of joy to look at yours!

PART 4

THE
WORLD
OF
MONEY

How does the economy affect my money?

Politicians and economists concentrate very heavily on economic growth. They are particularly concerned with **gross domestic product** (GDP). This is the monetary value of all goods and services produced within a country in a specific time period. The rate of GDP growth over any given time profoundly influences the job market, house prices, savings rates and borrowing costs.

Another major influence in our personal finances is the rate of **inflation** at any given time. Inflation refers to a sustained increase over time in the price of goods and services. If, for example, the rate of price inflation is 4 per cent, this means that you will need £104 to buy the same goods and services next year that you can buy this year with £100.

Inflation in the UK fell to zero in 2015. That was good news for savers, as it meant that for the first time in years, savers were getting a 'real' (i.e. above-inflation) return on their hard-earned cash. However **deflation**, when prices are sliding, can also be bad for the economy because it causes people to delay purchases in the hope that things get even cheaper. So, central banks and policymakers have to constantly walk a tightrope.

One big reason to watch out for inflation is that it can erode your living standards. Say you receive a salary boost after twelve months in a job. Your wage goes up 5 per cent from £20,000 to £21,000. If inflation over that time also went up 5 per cent, your new salary in real terms is still £20,000. It has only matched inflation – so you are no better off in reality.

This has indeed been the status quo for many households in recent times. Although average pay has gone up, it didn't match the rising cost of household essentials, notably energy and food. Some argue that people – as a result – have lower living standards now than they did before the recession. But others believe that incomes have also struggled to keep up with our aspirations, and the typical basket of goods we 'need' grows ever bigger.

The Office for National Statistics regularly changes the list of goods now considered mainstays of the British shopping basket. Here are some recent additions:

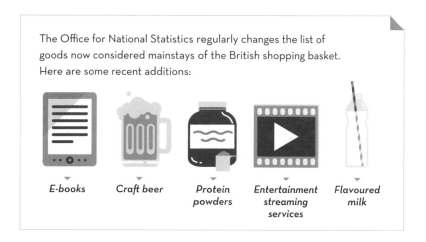

E-books   Craft beer   Protein powders   Entertainment streaming services   Flavoured milk

Debt

Some people have spent above their income in recent years to maintain what they think is a good quality of life. How has this been possible? One word: debt. Households in the UK in early 2015 owed an average £6,300 on top of their mortgages, taking on an extra £1.2 billion of debt in one month alone.

All of this suits the banks. Debt is central to how they make money. Their profits are based on what's called the **net interest margin**. This is the gap between the rate they charge borrowers and the rate they pay savers.

Credit and store cards typically allow you to borrow over 55 days at 0 per cent – but only if you pay it all back straightaway. A third of people incur NO interest on their credit cards and store cards by paying off their balance in full every month. These canny souls are known in the industry as **transactors**. Whereas the two-thirds of people who DON'T pay off their balance and incur interest are nicknamed **revolvers**.

But at least credit card/store card providers give you the option to avoid interest. You ALWAYS have to pay interest on mortgages, personal loans and payday loans. The only other exception is an interest-free overdraft on your bank account, but it is not common and typically has a limit of £200.

I'M LIVING SO FAR BEYOND MY INCOME THAT WE MAY ALMOST BE SAID TO BE LIVING APART.

– E.E. Cummings

The interest rate you pay is also determined by how long you borrow for. Remember the table in Chapter 1 (page 21)? It showed that the lower your repayments, the more interest will keep on rolling up, the longer you will be in debt and – importantly – the more you will pay the bank overall. The same goes for personal loans, which are used for big-ticket items like cars and home improvements. The bank will offer you a better rate over five years than it will over three years. Your repayments will look smaller but the bank will have to show you, in an illustration, how much you will REALLY pay overall. Pay close attention to these figures.

Peek into the crystal ball

The interest rates that are set by lenders in the UK are tied to the Bank of England's **base rate**. This is the rate at which the Bank of England will lend to financial institutions. Consequently, this base rate sets the tone for interest rates attached to many, but not all, financial products. So, for instance, mortgages and personal loans are heavily tied to the Bank of England base rate. But credit cards, store cards and payday loans are a different story. Credit cards typically charge 20 per cent, store cards 25–30 per cent and payday loans over 1,000 per cent.

You may see coverage in the news from time to time about whether the Bank of England base rate will rise, fall or stay the same. This debate matters a great deal to people who have mortgages. That is because they have to decide whether to take out a fixed-rate or tracker/variable mortgage.

If you're on a **fixed-rate mortgage**, the amount of interest you pay stays the same throughout the term of the deal, regardless of what the base rate does.

But if you're on a **tracker mortgage**, the interest you pay moves in parallel with the base rate, with the potential to go up or down. A **variable rate** will be influenced by the base rate, but is mostly determined by the bank itself.

So homeowners who think the base rate may rise in years to come will go for a fixed-rate deal, and this helps them if they're on a tight budget; they know exactly what they will pay for the duration of the deal. But those who think the bank rate will go low or stay the same for some time will take advantage and go for a tracker or variable rate.

Interest on debt in the UK is usually calculated as an **annual percentage rate** (APR). This standard figure gives you a total cost of the sum being borrowed and allows for comparison across the market. However, the rate you can get will depend on how 'risky' you are seen as a borrower. For instance, some products may advertise a rate that is only available to certain people, while some products may not be available to you at all. This could be due to your **credit rating** – a magic number set by an independent credit ratings agency, and checked by lenders, which indicates how 'credit-worthy' you are.

....

TIP ▸ *Paying a monthly subscription to a credit rating agency is not necessary – contrary to what they say! You can get a free copy of your credit rating, and you should always do this before applying for ANY kind of credit. You may not want to find out the real state of your credit rating, but you can be sure your lenders will – and if they don't like what they see, they can reject your application for credit, and damage your rating even further. So get to the truth before anyone else does and – if need be – you can repair your credit rating in good time.*

A BANK IS A PLACE THAT WILL LEND YOU MONEY IF YOU CAN PROVE THAT YOU DON'T NEED IT.

– Bob Hope

Are you a good or bad credit egg?

Here are some of the biggest factors which determine your credit status. In essence, they help lenders to decide whether you are a good egg or bad egg when it comes to your credit worthiness. Criteria range from the obvious – such as your previous track record in meeting loan repayments – to the obscure and surprising. It all helps to build a picture of your reliability as a borrower, indicating whether your finances are stable or potentially under lots of pressure.

FEATURES OF A GOOD CREDIT EGG

▸ Having a good or high level of household income
▸ Being in employment for a consistent period of time
▸ Owning your own home
▸ Being older
▸ Having fewer or no children
▸ Being in a professional job
▸ Having a bank account
▸ Having credit cards
▸ Being married
▸ Being on the electoral register

FEATURES OF A BAD CREDIT EGG

▸ Being divorced
▸ Being young
▸ Having a large number of dependants
▸ Living in rented accommodation
▸ Moving in and out of jobs
▸ Having limited existing access to banking facilities

....

TIP ▸ *Any application for credit will show up on your record, even if you are only browsing products. Always look for the 'no record' guarantee on any search.*

Playing the borrowing game

The fact is that we will ALL have to borrow money at some point in our lives. For instance, hardly any of us have the means to buy a home outright, so taking out a mortgage is usually essential. Likewise, debt is a fact of life for most university students due to higher-education costs these days. But student debt is probably one of the only examples where you have no choice about the interest you pay and – what's more – you probably shouldn't be too worried about it. In recent years, it has been one of the cheapest forms of borrowing around, with the debt set to be written off for many people who do not earn above a certain level. But that's the exception rather than the rule!

The two cardinal rules of debt are:
▸ Don't borrow money unless it will be used to enhance your life in the long term. A home, university education and car are potentially three good examples.
▸ If you have to borrow, try to limit how much.

For instance, dipping into an overdraft, even if it's approved, shouldn't become the norm: rates can vary and be very tricky to weigh up. Your bank may offer you an approved credit limit at a standard rate, but the Money Advice Service says this should only be used for emergencies. As for unapproved overdrafts ... don't go there!

The historian Tacitus saw the downsides of badly managed debt as far back as 33 CE. He described interest as an 'ingrained evil in the city of Rome, a very frequent cause of sedition and discord strongly disapproved of'.

Having a good credit rating helps enormously – some people establish a perfect repayment record on their credit cards solely for this purpose. But there are other ways to ensure that you don't pay over the odds to borrow:

① Switch your mortgage. Mortgages can usually be switched to new terms, and very often this can be a big money-saver. For instance, on a £150,000 British mortgage, where your starting rate was 4.53 per cent, you could save over £2,000 a year by switching it to a two-year fixed rate at 1.38 per cent, and then another two-year fix, and so on. Arrangement fees of £1,000 or more could eat into that and should be carefully weighed, as should any penalties for early switching.

② Shop around. Banks love to sell loans as 'extras' with other products. If you accepted a £5,000 loan from your bank over five years at 8.7 per cent, perhaps to buy a car, you would pay £100 a year (£500 in total) more than if you hunted down the best deal on the market at 5.3 per cent.

③ Don't be dazzled by promotional gimmicks. Banks have been offering air miles and even holidays as well as cashback deals to attract new mortgage business. But it is the combination of rates and fees that matters.

④ Go for a challenger. You may have been hearing a little bit about the rise of 'challenger' banks in recent years. These are small and mid-sized players trying to break the dominance of the big four banks in the UK. They're well worth considering if you're looking to borrow cheaply. At the start of 2015 in the UK the cost of borrowing £3,000 over two years was between £575 and £692 at the 'big four'. At the challenger banks? Between £362 and £456.

⑤ Go social. Borrowing that same amount with a big social lender such as Zopa or RateSetter costs even less – between £177 and £214. Peer-to-peer lending is a significant breakthrough in the financial industry, enabling borrowers and savers to bypass the banks by lending to each other and businesses.

⑥ Get out of your revolver rut! Take the opportunity, if you can, to transfer your credit-card balance to a no-interest deal and give yourself two or more years to pay it off. It could cost you as little as 2 per cent in fees, meaning a balance worth £3,000 would cost you only £60. This is called a zero per cent balance transfer and is a great ruse providing you can repay all of it by the end of the offer period.

⑦ Avoid payday loans like the plague. They can normally be approved within an hour (supposedly following credit checks). However, looking at the typical APR charged by this sector (normally over 1,000 per cent), it is clear you are paying a huge premium for this convenience. Although there are now caps on the fees attached to these loans in many countries, this has come too late for many unfortunate consumers whose failure to repay has jacked up their debt. Don't fall into this trap – careful budgeting and regular saving should normally avert the need for emergency injections of cash, and the huge interest that comes with it.

8 Don't forget the fees! This is especially the case with mortgages, where a seemingly attractive low fixed-rate deal can be a dead giveaway for a high arrangement fee. Also check whether interest is charged on a daily basis, which will be better for you than if charged on a monthly or annual basis.

....

TIP ▸ *If you use spare cash to pay off debt, always reduce your most expensive loan first.*

DEBT IS ONLY BEAUTIFUL AFTER IT IS REPAID.

– Russian proverb

Housing headaches

Housing has long been a cultural obsession in the UK. But it has also become a huge financial headache for the younger generation. Renting has become exorbitant, average deposits needed by first-time buyers have been rising and – most importantly – the supply of homes has not kept pace with demand, meaning homes are eye-wateringly expensive in some areas. If you DO make it onto the housing ladder, the costs don't stop there. You've got the demands of a mortgage and threat of repossession if you don't keep up with it, as well as insurance, maintenance, solicitors' fees and moving costs to consider.

Yet surveys suggest that, despite the barriers to home ownership, it is still most young people's dream. How come? Well, £2,400 a year is one reason. That's the average saving on buying, rather than renting, the same two-bedroom flat with a typical first-time mortgage, as website Zoopla reported in 2014. It found that in 86 per cent of cities in the UK it was, on average, 14 per cent more expensive to be a tenant than an owner.

There are also the obvious attractions of property as a long-term investment, especially when you consider the steady appreciation in house prices that many older people have enjoyed.

Initially, being a tenant is often cheaper than being an owner, as mortgage repayments tend to be higher than rental costs. But as long as you are steadily eating into your capital debt – mortgage payments come down, whereas rents inflate over time.

Sure, the buying process looks alarmingly expensive and the outlays are steep. But after 25 or 30 years, you should have nothing left to pay, while your renting counterparts will still (arguably) be throwing good money after bad.

After all, renting comes with some financial banana skins of its own. As well as forking out a typical deposit of £840, plus stumping up the first month's rent, almost half of UK renters pay an average £300 in fees to letting agents and landlords, according to SpareRoom.co.uk's 'True Cost of Renting' survey of more than 4000 flats and houses in 2014.

It means tenants are looking at typical upfront costs of £1,700 each time they move, including deposits which may not be refunded in full. Tenancy fees are legal (though not in Scotland) and must be published, but they can still be arbitrary. Negotiation and knowing your rights can help, but don't bank on it. If your property is in high demand, your landlord will always have the upper hand.

So if you dream of climbing on the property ladder, what can give you a leg-up?

1 Try a 'home saver' account. This pays a better savings rate if you are piling up the cash towards a deposit.

2 Turn to your family. Some banks offer family savings plans, where parents or grandparents can contribute. Guarantor mortgages allow parents to offer security where young borrowers don't yet earn enough. Staying at home can also be a real boon if you're trying to save for property, as many generous parents charge minimal or no rent. But always establish clear boundaries, rules and ways you can help out around the house from the outset. Otherwise, the family home quickly becomes a warzone!

3 Look for shared equity schemes. These are offered by builders of new homes, and sometimes by local authorities. This can be a game-changer, as you won't have to pay interest on the share of the equity you don't own.

4 Hunt down ex-local-authority homes or smaller properties. Some new developers have been building 'one-bedder' homes as a solution for first-time buyers. In 2015, Pocket Living began promoting designed compact starter homes on land bought from local authorities, available to local people earning below £66,000 and priced 20 per cent below market value.

5 Downsize your expectations. Never rule out the merits of moving to a cheaper part of the town or country.

One couple hit the headlines in 2014 for buying their first home in Stoke-on-Trent for just £1. They got this lucky break because their local council wanted to attract buyers to run-down areas. So the couple received a £30,000 loan to pay back over ten years in order to renovate the two-bedroomed mid-terrace property. Their home's value a year later? £70,000.

....

TIP ▶ *When it comes to a mortgage, you can make your savings sweat by going for an 'offset' product. First developed in Australia and now popular in the UK, offset mortgages work by offsetting your savings instantly against the amount you owe on your mortgage, so they only pay interest on the difference between the two. The double-whammy bonus is that you pay less interest on your debt, and less tax on your savings.*

Why the bank needs YOU to save

Of course, banks don't just want us to borrow money – they need us to save a fair amount too. That is because our deposits are used to lend out money on mortgages, loans and other forms of debt. But our bank may need our savings at some times more than others – and the **annual equivalent rate** (AER – i.e. the return you would get if your cash was left undisturbed in the account for 12 months) is directly affected by that.

IF SAVING MONEY IS WRONG, I DON'T WANT TO BE RIGHT!

– William Shatner

In recent times, banks in the UK have received funding from elsewhere, notably the Bank of England, so they haven't needed to offer juicy interest rates to reel in our deposits. Therefore, banks have tried to get away with paying as little as possible to savers, keeping that net interest margin as profitable as possible.

But you can still maximise the interest you earn on your savings – so long as you think of my savings seesaw:

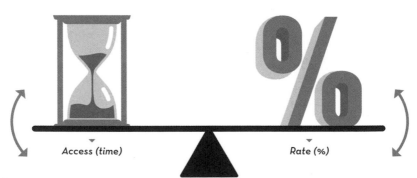

Access (time)   Rate (%)

Generally speaking, the more times you're allowed to withdraw your savings, the less interest you'll earn, and vice versa. When one side of the seesaw goes up, the other goes down.

So if you go low on access but high(er) on interest, you're looking at **fixed-rate bonds** and **notice accounts**, which require you to lock up money for two to five years. That is because the bank can make more use of longer-term deposits. On the plus side, they remove the temptation for you to pull the money out for spending (unless you want to pay a charge, that is). What's more, you're benefitting from interest being paid on the accumulating interest – this is commonly known as the magic of **compound interest**.

If you want to get more access to your account, you're looking at **limited withdrawal** and **instant access** accounts, both of them doing exactly what they say on the tin. But you're also dialling down the interest you earn, so these accounts will do very little for your cash in the long term.

The bank may try to win you over with a 'teaser' rate for a year or so. But this is a classic play on our inertia by the financial industry. Your bank relies on the fact that a sizeable proportion of customers will not bother to switch to another account a year later, or will forget, or will put it off. That's when the bank starts making its profit. Keep awake, and you can be a winner!

IF YOU WOULD BE WEALTHY, THINK OF SAVING, AS WELL AS GETTING.

- Benjamin Franklin

Free money

Gambling has become a national pastime in the UK, with betting companies falling over each other to get new customers. They offer a 'free bet' of perhaps £25 to get people hooked. According to one industry agency, they are prepared to spend up to £300 to get a new customer!

But we all know what happens when gambling gets out of hand. The way to avoid this slippery slope is to look at all 'free money' with suspicion. And that doesn't just go for betting shops and casinos. Banks may dangle incentives like hard cash – up to £150 in the UK in 2015 – to persuade their rivals' customers to defect and open new current accounts with them. That is because the bank hopes to make money in the long run. How? While all UK banks still offer free banking, many are successfully switching growing numbers of their customers – one in four now – to fee-paying accounts offering perks and extras.

....

TIP ▶ *Never pay a fee for banking in exchange for insurance and other perks without being sure you need them, don't already have them or know what they are really worth.*

Who takes on your risk?

There is a dizzying array of insurance policies available on the market – not least because they are very lucrative money-spinners for the financial sector. However, only one insurance is legally required in the UK: third-party car insurance – though mortgage lenders will want you to have buildings insurance. That leaves a huge assortment of policies that we can take or leave.

The idea behind insurance is that you pool risk among a large group of individuals by getting them to pay a monthly or annual premium, building up a fund which is used to pay out claims for events covered by the policy. Insurance firms carefully calibrate the level of your premiums based on the likelihood of claims.

In some types of insurance, how much you pay may be highly attuned to the level of risk you personally present. For instance, health insurers

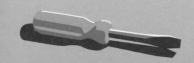

will want to know every detail of your medical records, charging you high premiums if you have ill health. But, elsewhere, insurers take a one-size-fits-all approach. Phone insurers will treat you and your mate exactly the same, even if you know he is far more likely to lose his phone than you are. You might be wondering whether you should pay the same rate – or have the insurance at all.

It all depends on which disasters you *think* are most likely to befall you. Not all insurance is needed by everybody all of the time – far from it. It's a fine balance between keeping the costs low and maintaining a reasonable safety net. You've got to ask: can I accept some risks myself without paying an insurance company to do it?

Research by consumer group Which? in 2013 found that two of the latest Sony and Panasonic TVs have only a 3–6 per cent chance of breaking down in the first five years. At the three biggest electrical outlets you would have to pay between 31 per cent and 38 per cent of the purchase price to buy an 'extended warranty' on one of those sets for between one to five years, or from £160 to £230. Yet in the unlikely event of a power supply or frame problem, a repair should cost £50 to £100 at most.

Which? also found the same trap with extended warranties for washing machines. Here the five-year 'peace of mind' would hike the cost of buying a new Bosch or Hotpoint machine by between 45 per cent and 60 per cent. Hotpoint had a 26 per cent breakdown probability, and Bosch only 12 per cent.

Money motivator

What are the ten most important things in your life that would cost you money if they were lost or damaged?

Mine might be: *What would yours be?*

① My health   ① .... ☐
② My flat   ② .... ☐
③ My cellos   ③ .... ☐
④ My laptop   ④ .... ☐
⑤ My car   ⑤ .... ☐
⑥ My smartphone   ⑥ .... ☐
⑦ My TV   ⑦ .... ☐
⑧ My washing machine ⑧ .... ☐
⑨ My personal music player ⑨ .... ☐
⑩ My travelpass/card ⑩ .... ☐

Now tick all those where you have an insurance or warranty plan of some kind. How many ticks do you have?

I ticked five, and here are my blanks:

▶ **My health:** I have no insurance for my health – I'm self-employed, and I tend to believe I simply have to look after myself. If you are a full-time employee, you might still be happy to rely on yourself. If you feel this is tempting providence, you need to think about how much it costs to insure your health, or your life, and what sort of bargain it is. How much do I save by not having this cover? £240 a year for income protection.

▶ **My laptop:** I am working on the basis that laptops wear out and get out of date within an ever-shorter time, but are (in my experience) pretty reliable. I would rather be careful, and save up the money I might have paid on an insurance premium towards my next model. These days you can back up your important files and music quite easily – so look into

the cheapest way of doing that. Saving? Around £60 per year.

▶ *My TV:* I have a new TV with a one-year warranty. On this one, I'm following the same principle as with my laptop. I inherited my previous set from my late grandma, and after a while decided to cancel the insurance on it. The TV lasted eighteen months before it started to go on the blink. Saving? Around £150 a year.

▶ *My washing machine:* I had a warranty on the machine inherited with my flat, and have used it for a serious repair. But I know there is perhaps only one major other part that could need replacing. I decided to stop the warranty and go out and get the new model when I have to. Saving so far? Around £150 a year.

▶ *My music player:* OK, I don't want to lose it, but I have a bargain model which costs less than £50 to replace, and the important stuff is on my laptop. Saving? £50 a year.

In conclusion, I could easily be paying out £650 on an annual basis for insurance I don't really need when I should try to be careful and absorb as much of the risk myself anyway.

However, sometimes insurance just can't be avoided. Remember my cardinal debt rules? Similar principles apply here. If you have to cover your back, make sure you pay as little as possible. That means making a date in your diary to look for cheaper deals when your existing policy comes up for renewal. It's almost impossible *not* to save a substantial sum on your car insurance renewal. Be careful, though. Paying less often means having less cover, which can nullify a lot of potential claims; this is not always apparent when you take out a policy. Read the small print carefully so you understand what is – and isn't – covered by the policy.

....

TIP ▶ *You can save bundles on your insurance by not just going on a price-comparison site but phoning up specialist brokers to get an even better deal. That is because they can ask you questions that may help the actuary (i.e. the number cruncher) decide you are lower risk and can pay less.*

THERE ARE WORSE THINGS IN LIFE THAN DEATH. HAVE YOU EVER SPENT THE EVENING WITH AN INSURANCE SALESMAN?

– Woody Allen

The Columbo moment ('Just one more thing …')

Beware the sales culture in our stores that means there is always a little insurance 'add-on' waiting for you.

Insurance has to be sold, otherwise we wouldn't go out and buy it. So insurance is often put in front of us as we are buying a consumer item – be it a coffee machine, a flat-screen TV or a new smart phone. The bigger the item, the more likely customers are to say 'yes' – hence the statutory fourteen-day 'cooling-off period' in the UK for financial transactions.

If a TV has cost several hundred pounds, it can make the £15-a-month back-up plan sound so reasonable, especially when you are on a retail high and you don't want to offend the lovely salesperson.

Similarly, the car showroom can be a highly seductive environment. Anyone buying a new car will find a menu of potential add-ons put in front of them, from rust protection to luxury fittings, whose prices look small alongside the big number you have already decided to part with. But you probably don't need them and would never have thought about them until the 'need was created'.

The biggest purchase of your life – your home – really takes the biscuit. The mis-selling of **payment protection insurance** (PPI) has led to £25 billion being repaid to UK bank customers over the past few years, and much of it was sold to people signing on the dotted line for a mortgage. The 'point of sale' pressure to say yes to something small, because people's attention was on the big prize, combined with the gratitude to the bank for giving it to them, prompted the biggest add-on insurance scandal in modern times.

The rest of the unneeded PPI was sold to people worried about whether they might fall down on credit-card payments. But for most of them, unaware of what they had really signed up to, it just added huge amounts of extra repayment to their monthly interest bills. Few policies ever paid out.

Here comes the bride (and the bill)

Weddings are big business these days. In Scotland alone, they contributed £537 million to the economy in 2013. It is no wonder that a whole industry now exists solely to whip up aspirations and charge a hefty sum to deliver them. You might not realise that many venues hike up prices the minute you mention the 'w' word when booking.

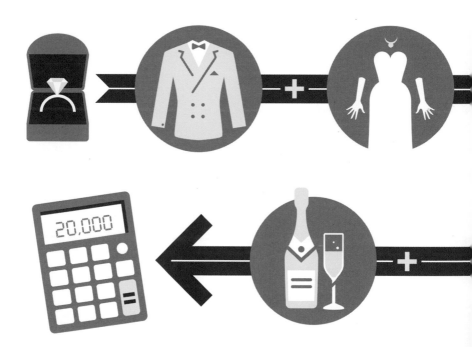

A frequently quoted cost for a typical wedding in the UK is £20,000. But not all lovebirds are breaking the bank. One in three British couples saves money by getting married in autumn or winter, according to a 2015 poll conducted by AA Financial Services. This strategy can chop as much as £2,000 off the total bill.

A quarter of couples also kept within budget by having a midweek or Sunday ceremony. No wonder, since many pubs and restaurants let you hire them out for free during this time as long as their guests spend a certain amount behind the bar. Another 19 per cent made their own cake and table decorations, 15 per cent delayed or went on a budget honeymoon, 12 per cent wore a vintage dress or suit and 7 per cent got married abroad.

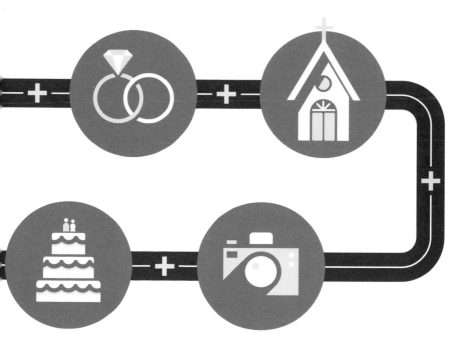

....

TIP ▶ *Learn the art of haggling. Clever wedding planners pit merchants against one another and drive down quotes in the process. Once a firm knows that you can quite easily go elsewhere, they may be less inclined to take you for a ride.*

The longevity conundrum

When pensions were first introduced to Britain in 1909, they were only available for those aged over 70 and paid 5 shillings a week – equivalent to £23 in today's money. Plus, anyone wanting this pension would have to pass a test to prove they had 'good character'!

In the early 20th century, you weren't really expected to have a long retirement (if any!) due to low life expectancy. Today, it's a very different story. Almost a quarter of the UK population will be over 65 by 2030 and a third of babies born in 2013 could live to 100 according to a survey by Towers Watson. So governments are slowly upping the state pension age, putting the onus on us to save more for the future. The financial industry is also persuading us to put every spare penny we have into either an occupational pension scheme (one offered by an employer) or a private pension (one taken out by individuals with financial firms). The common argument is that the earlier you start, the more chance you have that your monthly contributions will be invested long enough by fund managers to be transformed into a pot of gold – all thanks to the magic of the stock market.

RISING LIFE EXPECTANCY

DATE BORN	LIFE EXPECTANCY FOR MEN	LIFE EXPECTANCY FOR WOMEN
1901	45	49
1951	66	70
2010	78	82
2030	86	88

A pension is essentially a one-way safe – you can put money in but you can't get it out, at least not till later life. The government should reward you for your patience by providing decent tax relief. In the UK, basic rate (20 per cent) taxpayers will get £125 paid into their pension for every £100 they put in, because the £25 tax is not paid on the contribution. So it amounts to an uplift of 25 per cent. The incentive is even greater for higher rate (40 per cent) taxpayers – though that perk is constantly liable to political change.

But pensions have got a bad rep because managers and financial advisers have opened up the safe all too often and creamed off a layer of charges from these captive funds that can seriously affect long-term returns. Also, people have rightly questioned whether there are more flexible ways to save for the long term using regular savings and investments. For instance, in New Zealand, first-time buyers have been allowed to access funds from their pension to get on the housing ladder as part of the Kiwi Saver Scheme.

So what options are available and how should they be weighed up? Take a look at my pensions decision tree over the page:

PENSIONS *(occupational and private)*

Upsides: Get tax relief; are a much-needed safety net in retirement; and long-term investment can produce enough money for retirement.

Downsides: They can't be accessed until retirement; charges can eat into the fund; and there is no guaranteed estimate of fund's worth at retirement because you take on all the risk.

OCCUPATIONAL

(i.e. workplace) pension scheme (most likely to be a defined contribution scheme)

Upsides: Get contributions from your employer; you don't need to make any effort to save; and regulations are helping to tighten up how the schemes are run.

Downsides: Contributions made by you and the employer may be inadequate; there is little or no choice about the scheme chosen by the employer; and you risk leaving pension pots stranded in different plans and all racking up charges if you move jobs frequently.

PRIVATE PENSION PLAN

(sold by big pension firms)

Upsides: Good for the self-employed who can't access workplace schemes; a top-up for potentially inadequate workplace pension pots; there is lots of choice about where to invest; there's the potential to reduce charges if you shop around; and you can choose how much you invest.

Downsides: You take on the responsibility for choosing the best plan unless you pay for an independent financial adviser. Independent online advice sites can offer plenty of help and guidance if you don't want to pay for an adviser, but sites will never recommend a specific pension plan.

TIP ▸ *Charges have a big impact on the pension returns you will get and must be carefully compared. Look for the overall effect of charges on your pot each year, as they have to be explained.*

PART 5

YOUR
FINANCIAL
GOALS

Why we all need financial goals

What is your biggest financial dream? If you're a young adult living at home, it might simply be the journey to financial independence. If you're paying high rent, it could well be getting your own place. Someone in the early stages of their career might long for a comfortable standard of living, while someone further down the track may want to have a well-earned retirement. Others may simply aspire to stop living hand-to-mouth and going from one cash-flow emergency to the next. The more financially secure among us might be focused on higher matters – finding ways to make a difference in the world.

What all these goals have in common is that they allow people a sense of freedom and autonomy in their lives. Having money gives people more options, more choice. And that is why money, or rather the careful management of it, is a worthwhile end in itself. Because you may be sat there, wondering what on earth your future will look like and concerned only with having enough for tomorrow's crazy night out. But, as Aristotle said, you want the means to satisfy a new desire – whenever it may arise.

> **MONEY IS A GUARANTEE THAT WE MAY HAVE WHAT WE WANT IN THE FUTURE. THOUGH WE NEED NOTHING AT THE MOMENT IT INSURES THE POSSIBILITY OF SATISFYING A NEW DESIRE WHEN IT ARISES.**
>
> *– Aristotle*

Be your own financial adviser

Goals are the bread and butter of professional financial advisers. Their ability to sketch out your dreams and tell you how to realise them is what makes their services so valuable. Sadly, it may only be available for the more affluent. Financial planners in the UK will often expect you to have at least £100,000 to play with. So most of us will have to become our own financial advisers. What does this involve?

Well, at its most simple, financial advice is simply a four-stage process:

▸ Assess ▸ Decide ▸ Act ▸ Review

Assess

Assessing your current financial situation is everything. If you don't know what is coming in and going out, you aren't in position to make any plans for the future. So the first step is to draw up a budget. This is a breakdown of your income and your outgoings over a period of one month.

MONEY MOTIVATOR

Step 1: Gather your bank account and credit card statements – this is pretty much all the information you will need to figure out what is going on. You might want to look at the last two or three months in order to capture your typical pattern of earning and spending. After all, there may have been an exceptional occurrence that would skew the picture, such as spending in the run-up to Christmas. For bills that are not paid by direct debit, you need to figure out the monthly equivalent cost (i.e. divide the annual figure by 12).

Step 2: Get yourself pen and paper or a computer spreadsheet. Tot up all the spending items that belong in each of the categories on the budget I have provided below. So, for instance, all your separate supermarket bills would need to be added up to give you an aggregate food bill over the month/months.

Step 3: Once you have total figures for spending in each area, fill in the budget I have provided.

BUDGET

	INCOME (£)
Earnings after tax, National Insurance and other deductions	
Tax credits or Universal Credit	
Other benefits	
Other income	
TOTAL NET INCOME	

	OUTGOINGS (£)
Rent or mortgage	
Council tax	
Regular bills (gas, electricity, water)	
Phones, broadband, TV or entertainment subscriptions, TV licence	
Home insurance (contents, buildings)	
Food, drink and household goods	
Beauty products and treatments	
Clothing, accessories and footwear	
Travel (car insurance, petrol, rail, buses, other)	
Going out, nights in (alcohol, meals out, cinema, etc)	
Gym membership, exercise classes and sports	
Holidays	
Other leisure	
Credit card and loan repayments	
Charitable giving	
Other spending	
TOTAL EXPENDITURE	

Decide

Once you see how much you spend each month, you may get quite a shock! You may also start to understand why you get into debt so easily and why there is so little wriggle room to save for future ambitions. The question is: how comfortable are you with all aspects of your spending?

Deciding what is essential and non-essential (or discretionary) for your life can be a huge breakthrough, not only in making wise cuts to your spending but also making room for what really matters to you in the long run.

But this is easier said than done. For instance, we all have to eat, we can't walk about naked and we don't want to smell and look a total state. But it is fair to say that a meal at the most expensive restaurant in town, designer clothes and luxury toiletries are not really necessary – right? Here are my guidelines for working out what is financially essential in your life:

1 You can think of all your fixed expenses as being payments that you are contractually or legally obliged to meet. For instance, you'd be swiftly evicted if you couldn't make rent or meet your mortgage repayments and you'd be quickly chased by debt collectors if you started falling behind on gas, electricity and credit card repayments.

2 When considering each item, ask yourself: did I already have that item or something similar? Did I need a replacement in order to stay up and running?

3 Any expenses that keep your body, home and family running are clearly essential (sanitary products, cleaning supplies, childcare) but anything relating to entertainment, alcohol, home decoration, leisure and beauty can be considered non-essential.

4 Separate the food you tend to eat at home (like breakfast and dinner) from meals in restaurants or sandwiches from a cafe. Any food you buy in advance from a supermarket/grocery store could be considered essential, while any food bought and eaten 'on the go' falls under discretionary spending.

5 Transport is essential for most of us to get from A to B, but consider the difference between your commute to work and a taxi needed on a night out because you missed the last train/bus. And what about those trips by car at the weekend to the local shops? If you could walk instead, you might want to put some of your fuel costs in the discretionary column.

TO CUT OR NOT TO CUT ... THAT IS THE QUESTION

Now is the time to reinforce an important point. We don't want to remove every joy from our lives.

In recent years, I have come to question whether buying a cheeky latte from an oh-so-cool coffee shop every day is a good use of money. But for some people, that insanely complicated cup of coffee is a lifesaver, even if the effect is more psychological than physical. Who am I to say that this little caffeine boost isn't worth its weight in gold if it gets people through the day?

Here's what I say: if you've got your financial house in order, go for it. But that doesn't mean it isn't worth investigating cheaper options, or alternative ways of doing things. Most importantly, you have to be able to truly justify the luxury. Be individualistic in your financial decisions, aware of each purchase and what it does for you.

BUY ONLY SOMETHING THAT EXCITES YOU, NOT JUST FOR THE SIMPLE ACT OF SHOPPING.

- Karl Lagerfeld

COULD YOU LIVE ON 90 PER CENT?

Making any future goal happen – whether it's a first home, an exciting holiday or basic security in everyday life – relies on having a solid savings habit in place. The reason it is called a 'habit' is because it takes some deliberate practice to put away money, rather than spend it. However, with practice it becomes default behaviour – something you barely have

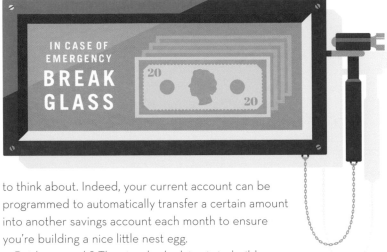

to think about. Indeed, your current account can be programmed to automatically transfer a certain amount into another savings account each month to ensure you're building a nice little nest egg.

But how much? The standard advice is to build a savings kitty equivalent to three month's income as a lifeline in emergencies. This means that you avoid having to borrow money (potentially at a high price if it's needed at short notice) and defaulting on any existing repayment commitments such as rent or a mortgage. Always make sure these savings go into an instant-access or (at a push) limited withdrawal account: you don't want to be forfeiting interest simply for taking out savings in your hour of need.

Once you have established your emergency kitty, you will need to consider putting money into a higher-earning account to help you save for loftier ambitions. You may be wondering how this is possible without compromising your standard of living. But ask yourself one question:

Could I live on 90 per cent of my disposable income today?

A great tip imparted by money guru Alvin Hall is: could you reduce the spending you have left over after bills and essential expenses by just 10 per cent and pop that spare money into a savings account? I bet you any money that this is possible. Well, actually, I WON'T bet you money, because gambling is one area where savings could be made. According to Sun Life, the annual average spend on betting in the UK is rising and stood at £140 in 2014. But a quarter of the population has less than £100 in savings.

So, just suppose you are Mr or Miss Average and you 'invest' £12 a month in lottery tickets, sweepstakes or other little flutters. Just think what that £12 a month could do in your rainy-day fund – £144 a year, £720 over five years, and that's *not* including interest.

....

TIP ▸ *Don't commit to a pension until you are in the savings habit and have at least built up an emergency fund. If you want to buy your first home, a tax-free savings account is the best option in the short term. From April 2016 in the UK, you are able to earn £1,000 a year in tax-free interest on top of Individual Savings Account allowances.*

_____

MAKING PLANS

When deciding what to do with your money, you may come across some classic pitfalls I alluded to in Chapter 1 of the book. With that in mind, here is some guidance:

▸ Be aware of your financial constraints. Can you realistically afford two weeks in the Caribbean every year as well as buying your own flat in ten years? Which matters most?
▸ Take it one step at a time. Reduce your outgoings (perhaps one area at a time) before you move on to savings, for instance.
▸ Make sure you get realistic (ideally conservative) estimates of how much you need for your goals so you have specific numbers in mind.
▸ Try to have a balance of short-term and long-term goals. Too much emphasis on one or the other is a recipe for trouble.
▸ Try to avoid goals that are driven mostly by outside expectations. They should make *you* happy.
▸ Set yourself realistic timeframes so that you are motivated to carry out the necessary steps.

Act

By now, you have (hopefully) made some broad financial decisions. These may include, but not be restricted to:

▸ Reducing debt ▸ Cutting back on certain non-essentials
▸ Finding ways to trim essential spending ▸ Saving more to meet certain goals

Now is the time to act. Knowing that you have to make changes is all fair and well, but you've got to put your money where your mouth is and behave differently. With that in mind, here are some specific areas that you can tackle to help make your financial dreams a reality ...

MONEY MOTIVATOR

Find yourself a pocket-sized notebook to use as a **spending diary**. Over the course of one month – perhaps from the day you get paid – list everything you spend!

Try to document every last item you buy, from light bulbs to concert tickets, noting when they were bought, how much they cost and *why* you bought them. It might be that the very act of accounting for each expense will stop you going ahead with certain purchases, however it is important to carry on as you normally would so you feel the full benefits of this exercise.

Do keep this up for a full month – if it's any less time you won't build up a decent picture of your spending habits.

THE TRUTH ABOUT COFFEE

Here are some amazing statistics to demonstrate our infatuation with coffee shops. According to Thinkmoney, in Britain alone, 16 per cent of adults visit a coffee shop five or more times a month, while 750,000 Brits go more than 20 times a month, spending over **£588** on average each year. In fact, 37 per cent of Brits spend more than £5 per visit. Guess which age group has fallen for coffee shops the most? Yep, the under 24s – over three-quarters of them go once a month and 22 per cent go at least once a week.

This chart illustrates the substantial savings we could make even if we just cut down, rather than cut out, our coffee-shop visits. Of course, even if you visit a coffee shop just three times a month, £88 is still a hefty annual sum – is it really worth it?

I HAVE MEASURED OUT MY LIFE WITH COFFEE SPOONS.

- T.S. Eliot

ANNUAL COST OF VISITING COFFEE SHOPS

(based on a medium latte from Costa, costing £2.45 a time)

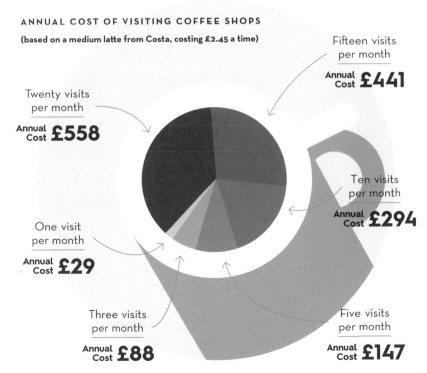

Fifteen visits
per month

Annual
Cost **£441**

Twenty visits
per month

Annual
Cost **£558**

Ten visits
per month

Annual
Cost **£294**

One visit
per month

Annual
Cost **£29**

Three visits
per month

Annual
Cost **£88**

Five visits
per month

Annual
Cost **£147**

EATING OUT AND SPENDING BIG

Often, 'essential' spending can take on epic proportions. Lunch is a major case in point. The average UK employee spends £90,000 on quick and easy lunches over the course of their working lives, according to 2013 research from Officebroker.com. For someone on a take-home pay of £2,000 a month that equates to almost four years of salary to pay for this luxury.

But what about the smarty-pants who make their own packed lunch AND bring homemade tea/coffee to work? Here is how the savings stack up.

COMPARATIVE COST OF LUNCHES

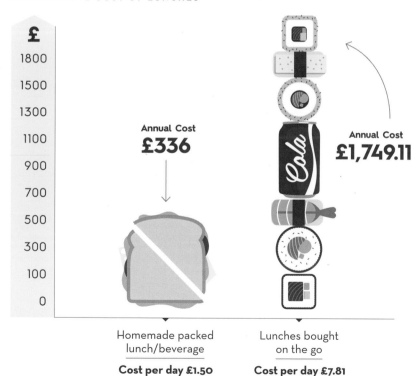

Annual Cost
£336

Annual Cost
£1,749.11

Homemade packed
lunch/beverage

Cost per day £1.50

Lunches bought
on the go

Cost per day £7.81

You could save more than £1,400 a year on lunch costs if you simply set aside time to prepare. Now there's an incentive to wake up fifteen minutes earlier. Planning ahead also means you might spurn sugary snacks and savoury pick-me-ups in favour of more wholesome food.

....

TIP ▸ *You don't have to make all your lunches from scratch – take some leftovers from last night's dinner and warm them up in the office. Get some Tupperware boxes and sandwich bags for this purpose. However, be warned: not all food can be reheated safely, so always check any labels.*

_____

LOOKING A MILLION DOLLARS ...

A 2014 study by beauty brand Feel Unique found that women will typically spend £100,000 on cosmetics over the course of their lives. Insanely, there are 54 items in the average, rather overstuffed, British make-up bag! Even men feel the pressure to (quite literally) keep up appearances. The high street chain Debenhams reckons that the average 30-year-old man spends around £100 a month on grooming.

But before you go out and pump any more money into the booming beauty business, ask yourself: do I already have this type of product at home? Have I completely used it up – i.e. cut the tube open or popped the bottom of the bottle in a cup of hot water and let it rest for a little while to get the last bit out? Did this fancy product really work the last time or can I 'trade down' to a cheaper brand to see if price makes that much difference?

What if you cut out a couple of products and used them less? For instance, many experts believe it is unnecessary to use cleanser on your face in the morning – a quick splash of water should do – while others doubt whether toner is necessary at all.

BEAUTY IS NOT CAUSED. IT IS.

– Emily Dickinson

Other ways to go from high to low maintenance include:

▸ Washing your hair only every few days to retain its natural oils.

▸ Only using concealer/foundation where it is strictly necessary.

▸ Using only face powder to reduce shine if you have great skin.

▸ Ditching hair dye wherever possible so hair can maintain its natural lustre.

▸ Using home remedies, such as cold teabags and cucumbers to depuff eyes, rather than shelling out on shop-bought products.

TAKE THE HOMEMADE CHALLENGE
For one month, see if you can substitute some expensive creams and sprays with all-natural ingredients already in your kitchen or store cupboard. These are some of my natural skin saviours:

▸ **Acne:** tea tree oil, witch hazel oil, crushed aspirin, sea or Epsom salts, calamine lotion

▸ **Dark circles:** cucumber, iced green tea bags

▸ **Dry skin:** honey, aloe vera, yoghurt, banana (made into a paste), evening primrose oil

▸ **Make-up remover:** jojoba oil

▸ **Dry hair:** coconut or jojoba oil (used sparingly)

WHY YOU SHOULDN'T CANCEL YOUR GYM MEMBERSHIP
Many couch dwellers vow to become gym bunnies when the clock strikes midnight on New Year's Eve. But if you've taken out gym membership in recent times, you may well be regretting your decision. Research by M&S Money has found that Brits waste a total of £632 million a month on gym memberships they never use and sport courses they never attend.

The standard advice is to cancel, especially when parks and pavements are free to pound. If only it were that simple! For starters, most gyms tie you into 12- or even 24-month contracts and make it very difficult for you to quit. Even if the contract is due to expire, you may have to give 30 days' notice or you are locked in for another year. People who try to cancel their direct debit without letting their gym know could even be chased by debt collectors and see their credit score suffer – an experience no one wants.

But there is a simple solution – use the gym. Membership is only a waste of money if it is never used. If you are paying a monthly fee, work out how much you are paying per visit at the moment. Then commit to going at least two or three times more often. Think of the cost per visit, which will drop dramatically. If you pay £45 a month every month and only go twice, you spend £22.50 per visit. That's an expensive run on the treadmill. But if you go once a week – that's just two more times – you pay half the amount at £10.38. Here's how much you save by going to the gym when you have membership – even you only use the steam room or cafe!

COST PER VISIT TO THE GYM

(based on a fee of £45 per month)

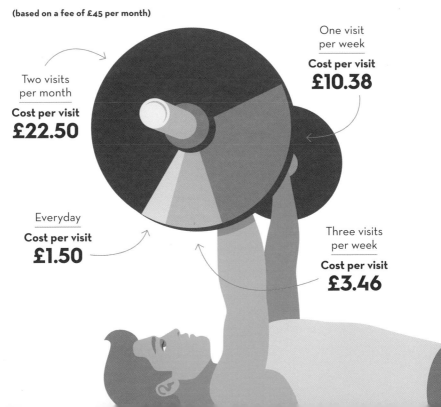

One visit
per week

Cost per visit

£10.38

Two visits
per month

Cost per visit

£22.50

Everyday

Cost per visit

£1.50

Three visits
per week

Cost per visit

£3.46

Many gyms also offer free personal trainers and free classes, which can be considerably better value than those offered by individual studios. Have a kit bag prepared at home or work to reduce hassle. If you are still not satisfied that you're getting value for money, check your contract or ask your gym to confirm when your membership expires *and* when you should give notice. Make a note in your diary and investigate cheaper alternatives. Check out pay-as-you-go and local-authority gyms for a better deal.

EATING WELL: THE SLOW COOKER IS YOUR FRIEND ...

Many people rightly aspire to have a healthier diet. But they also labour under the illusion that eating well costs more. Nothing could be further from the truth. We actually pay over the odds for convenient junk – and by a big margin. Research by website vouchercodes.co.uk has revealed that the average Brit buys twelve takeaways a month, at a cost of £110 a month. That adds up to £1,320 a year.

It doesn't have to be this way. Cooking healthy, varied meals doesn't just make your money go further. A well-stocked fridge, and using it to knock up a hearty meal from scratch, makes a tremendous difference to your quality of life, whatever your income.

If you're time-poor or lacking imagination when it comes to food – and I frequently have both problems – then the slow cooker is your best friend. A slow cooker allows you to prepare all of the following in the morning before you head to work:

▸ *Stews* ▸ *Soups* ▸ *Sauces* ▸ *Hot dips*

Use cheaper cuts of meat or fish (never mix the two), lots of vegetables and any passata, stock, sauces or spreads you have in the cupboard.

....

TIP ▸ *Anchovies are the one type of fish that work well in meat stews. Snip them up finely with scissors.*

By the time you return home, you'll have the basis for a healthy meal that can be eaten straight away. You can add pasta, rice, tapas or naan bread, or just eat the contents of the cook pot on its own. Make sure the cook pot is on a slow or low heat setting so it doesn't burn, and do follow the cooker's safety guidelines.

WELCOME TO THE CAPSULE FRIDGE

To have a healthy, low-cost diet, you'll need the right ingredients in your kitchen. Women will know that a capsule wardrobe consists of only a few classic items of clothing that are interchangeable, so you can mix and match individual items to your heart's content. Well, a capsule fridge is very similar. It always contains essential, healthy ingredients that go well with one another so you make cooking easy, and even fun.

Ditch the recipe book and start experimenting with your own DIY meals – you may discover an untapped talent!

THE STAPLES OF A CAPSULE FRIDGE AND STORE CUPBOARD

▶ **Meat & Fish:** Ham, smoked salmon, salmon steaks, fish cakes, cooked chicken, bacon bits, tuna, anchovies

▶ **Vegetables:** Cucumber, salad, onions, tinned tomatoes, spring onions, peppers, avocado, celery, carrots, peas

▶ **Extras:** Olives, potatoes, rice, couscous, hummus, yoghurt, pesto, herbs, pasta, sauces, stock cubes, cooking wine, rice, pulses, beans

TIP ▶ *The simple Mediterranean diet based on these ingredients has been found to ward off heart attacks, diabetes and even some types of cancer, according to Dr Catherine Itsiopoulos of La Trobe University in Melbourne.*

....

TIP ▶ *Always make time for a weekly shop, as ad hoc trips to the supermarket are rarely good value in the grand scheme of things. Take a shopping list to ensure you're not swayed by offers, illusory deals or impulse buys. Be sure to compare the unit price of food and only buy in bulk (using three-for-two or buy-one-get-one-free offers) if the item is on your list and sure to be eaten up.*

HOLISTIC GOALS

There are money-saving strategies that will allow you to kill lots of birds with one stone. They will really turbo-charge your motivation and help you stick to good habits.

You don't have to be good with maths to be good with money: here are some simple equations that anyone can understand! I dare you to come up with a few of your own.

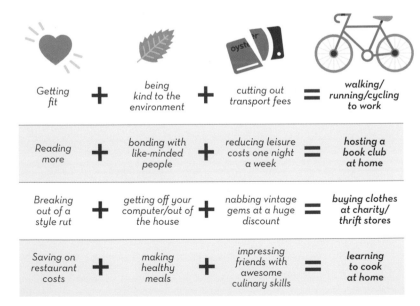

Getting fit	**+**	being kind to the environment	**+**	cutting out transport fees	**=**	walking/ running/cycling to work
Reading more	**+**	bonding with like-minded people	**+**	reducing leisure costs one night a week	**=**	hosting a book club at home
Breaking out of a style rut	**+**	getting off your computer/out of the house	**+**	nabbing vintage gems at a huge discount	**=**	buying clothes at charity/ thrift stores
Saving on restaurant costs	**+**	making healthy meals	**+**	impressing friends with awesome culinary skills	**=**	learning to cook at home

How many more can you dream up? Write them down here:

....

....

....

....

SPENDING CONFESSIONAL

Take time out once a month to study your spending diary, and think about some of the reasons why you are buying. Then, check each non-essential item against the following list. Which category best describes the reason for your purchase? Keep a tally next to each category and you'll quickly see where problems are occurring.

1 You're having a dreadful day. You've missed a deadline, a car drove into a puddle right next to you ... why not buy something to perk you up? **(The pick-me-up spender).**

2 You're in a hurry. You missed breakfast, so you'll grab something on the way to work. You have a wedding in two days' time so you'll race down to the shops or quickly go online to buy a new outfit. **(The hurried spender)**

3 You can't resist an offer. Buy one, get one free? Don't mind if I do! **(The promo spender).**

4 You find it difficult to walk past a shop or go online without spending money. **(The magnet spender).**

5 You want to get something specific but end up buying much more than you intend. **(The unintentional spender).**

6 It's payday – time to splash the cash! **(The payday spender).**

7 You really don't want to miss out. Your friends or partner invite you out for the evening. **(The FOMO – fear of missing out – spender).**

Which spender type are you? You probably fall into a combination of these categories but lean more heavily towards one. Being aware of the emotional factors behind your urge to splurge is crucial. That is the first step towards preventing 'kamikaze' shopping – i.e. emotion-fuelled spending sprees that leave you feeling guilty and ashamed. Knowing WHY you buy allows you to catch yourself mid-habit.

ALTERNATIVES TO RETAIL THERAPY

The problem is that retail therapy can seem ... well, very therapeutic!

But there is no substitute for *real* therapy, whatever that means for you. You may need professional help if you fit two or more of the following categories:

▸ You frequently buy products that you never use (even the price tags remain attached).
▸ You get a thrill from buying but feel depressed, guilty and shameful afterwards.
▸ You experience emotional 'blackouts' where you can't even remember what you've bought.
▸ You hide your purchases from other people you live with.
▸ You find yourself denying that you have a problem when confronted by others.
▸ You're getting into debt but you can't stop shopping.

An addiction to spending is like an addiction to drugs or alcohol. It can mar your life unless you face up to it and tackle it head on. A counsellor can help you identify the deep-seated reasons for your shopping compulsion and work with you to establish strategies for dealing with it. Ask your doctor or go online to find out what therapeutic services are available in your area. You won't be sorry!

Extreme spending can also be a symptom of bipolar disorder, so don't be afraid to find out if there's a bigger issue at play.

Of course, more minor forms of shopping addiction can be self-treated. Exercising, mending things, getting back to nature, being creative ... it totally depends on your psychological make-up and what makes YOU tick.

Former boxer Mike Tyson filed for bankruptcy in 2003 after overspending on houses, cars and even tigers. He later admitted that his habits left him 'destitute and broke'.

DECOY FREEBIES

Go back to the lists of your values and the activities you most enjoy that you wrote down on page 34.

Did you say that you value 'giving back' but don't actually do any volunteering? Do you value your friends but only see them once in a blue moon? Also, take a look at what you get pleasure from each week. Does it revolve around spending money? Is it aimed at keeping up appearances?

Now write down as many alluring activities as you can think of that involve little or no money. Be as imaginative as possible. One immediately springs to mind ... sorry, I'll behave myself. Now pick five that appeal to you most. Choose a combination of:

▶ Tried-and-tested treats (satisfying alternatives to spending that make you feel great – perhaps a movie night, a yoga session or playing your guitar).
▶ Easy activities that can be picked up instantly (so you can turn to these the second you have the urge to splurge – e.g. reading a book, going for a walk or listening to your favourite songs).
▶ New challenges that take you out of your comfort zone (look for productive pursuits that you can get your teeth into – e.g. starting a blog, re-organising your bedroom or researching opportunities to develop your career).

You can photocopy, write on and print off this list to keep by your side. These are your decoy freebies.

1 .... **4** ....

2 .... **5** ....

3 ....

CAUTION: I have deliberately excluded activities like 'watching TV' or 'browsing online' from my suggested list. These are classic ways for us to 'kill' time if we are not being active enough in our lives. I'm not saying we should banish TV and the internet from our lives altogether, but passivity can lead us to fall back into bad spending habits and make us more susceptible to commercial pressures.

'BUY NOTHING' DAY

Take a look at your diary over the next two weeks and pick ONE day which won't be unusually stressful or demanding. Could you do *only* your decoy freebies?

See how it goes. If you hate and it and find it to be a terrible deprivation, that will be eye-opening in itself. But, chances are, you may find it strangely liberating and enjoyable.

WATCH OUT: Often, people use the excuse of a new hobby to buy lots of expensive equipment and clothes. Is the pricey guitar or hiking gear REALLY going to help you keep up the commitment? Remember, you could borrow the necessary equipment from a friend or rent it through a website while you're trying things out. Let's face it, yoga will have the same benefits whether it is executed in top-of-the-range pants or a cheap pair of leggings found in the back of the wardrobe. Take advantage of free classes and 40-day taster trials to cut costs while you discover new interests that fire you up.

A DIFFERENT WAY OF LIFE ...

Several philosophies have sprung up in response to our overly monetised world in recent years. See if you might relate to some of them!

Minimalism

Otherwise known as tech nomads, modern-day minimalists prefer to keep their belongings to a minimum, possessing only as much as can fit in a backpack.

Dip your toe in the water by looking at your existing 'clutter' and asking yourself whether some of it has outlived its purpose. Once you've decided to part with your items, there are many ways to gain financially from de-cluttering:

▸ See whether some of your possessions could be sold in a virtual/real marketplace, through classified ads or in an auction.
▸ Local classified sites, which allow items to be picked up locally, often work out cheaper for both buyer and seller.
▸ Do not discount the potential value of faulty electrical goods, quirky clothing and strange goods – people find all kinds of uses for them.
▸ Items still in their packaging or with their tags on are particularly coveted.
▸ When trading in possessions online, don't accept the first price you are offered – get valuations from different places and spend some time compiling the best prices offered for each item. That way, you can double or even triple the money you get.

If items prove hard to shift, you can try swapping online instead, selling to friends and family or giving away unexpected presents throughout the year – you don't have to put a price on everything! Alternatively, you can donate to your local charity/thrift store or use a free recycling scheme such as Freecycle or Freeshare to minimise waste.

IT IS PREOCCUPATION WITH POSSESSIONS, MORE THAN ANYTHING ELSE, THAT PREVENTS US FROM LIVING FREELY AND NOBLY.

– Bertrand Russell

....

TIP ▶ *A favourite trick of mine is to buy second-hand good-quality DVDs and other items from local charity shops, where prices are vastly reduced, and return them shortly after they've been used. I've nabbed a bargain, paid no postage or selling fees, been kind to the environment and kept my home free of clutter. Win-win.*

Experientialism

This is very similar to minimalism, with the emphasis firmly on collecting incredible experiences rather than fancy items.

MONEY CAN'T BUY LIFE.

- Bob Marley

You don't have to splash the cash to have a good time. Here are some suggestions for memorable experiences on a budget:

▶ Refuse to do business with opportunistic ticket touts and only buy tickets at or below their original value from genuine fans who can't make the show. Many event promoters build up hype for big events before tickets go on sale, but a surprising number fail to sell out. So wait a few weeks to see if cheaper tickets become available online. A limited number of tickets may also be sold at knock-down prices on the day of the performance. Always compare different agencies and try to pick up tickets in person if possible to save postage and booking fees.

▶ Outdoor nature reserves, botanic gardens and parks are wonderful destinations for picnics or even camping trips.

▶ Under-26s can often access fantastic theatre, art and other cultural events for free or at a massive discount if they know where to look.

▶ Volunteering at music and book festivals can be a great way to meet new people and enjoy culture for nothing.

▸ Local festivals, gigs and comedy nights showcase fantastic new talent at very low prices.

▸ Look out for your favourite artists doing DJ or acoustic sets – these quirky events may be less pricey and perhaps more interesting than a full-blown concert.

▸ Students at local universities and colleges put on stunning degree shows, from exhibitions to fashion extravaganzas, which may be free or very cheap.

▸ Museums and art galleries often host free and fascinating events, from art classes to silent discos, to draw in punters.

▸ Signing up to a film-preview service gives you the opportunity to check out movie releases ahead of time for nothing. There are also certain days (like Tuesday) when cinema tickets tend to cost much less. Never buy popcorn, sweets and drinks from the cinema kiosk, where huge mark-ups can be expected – buy in advance to make huge savings.

▸ Your local council or community college may offer free and fun courses that provide an opportunity to meet like-minded people.

▸ Top attractions such as theme parks can offer two-for-one or discounted tickets at off-peak times.

Review

Every month, you need to reassess what you're doing and why you're doing it. Have there been any changes in your life since you put together your original action plan? For instance, have you seen your income go up, down or out the window? Have you met the love of your life or just hit Heartache Avenue? Are your spending and saving decisions working out reasonably well? Have you gone too far in any area ... and found out something that you've given up really isn't worth the pain?

It goes without saying that the budget needs to be a monthly exercise to keep on top of all the changes you're making, so be prepared to spend a little bit of time on it (especially at the beginning).

You also need to keep an eye on the news to see if the cost of small and big items has changed in recent times or if inflation/interest rates need to be considered afresh (see page 50).

MONEY IS ONLY A TOOL. IT WILL TAKE YOU WHEREVER YOU WISH, BUT IT WILL NOT REPLACE YOU AS THE DRIVER.

- Ayn Rand

TIP ▸ *Put dates relating to the end of your insurance policies, teaser rates and energy/broadband tariffs next to the item in each monthly budget – it will keep reminding you to take action in good time. Better still, make an entry in your calendar.*

PART 6

MONEY AROUND OTHERS

Our friends and families are the bedrock of our lives but they can also pose a big threat to our financial well-being without even knowing it. This chapter shows you how to manage your money with other people in mind so you can have fun, enjoy satisfying relationships and prevent discord – all while keeping your financial aspirations on track.

Everyone is different

Keep in mind that every individual has their own unique financial situation. To paraphrase Shakespeare, some are born wealthy, some achieve wealth and some have wealth thrust upon them. Some people are well-off by virtue of their career or family, and others have money due to unforeseen events, like a legacy or legal compensation from an accident.

I have learned to say 'no' to some more expensive social invitations, knowing that I'll be more critical of the value being offered and less likely to enjoy myself. Likewise, I have learned to be sensitive towards friends who don't earn a lot or find themselves in difficult financial circumstances. I find cheap and free things to do with those people so they don't believe our friendship has to come with a big price tag.

BE PROACTIVE
One of the best ways to avoid spending more than you would like is to assume the role of planner. This takes more time and effort but could save you a lot of dissatisfaction (and money) in the long run. Be the one to suggest cheaper venues, restaurants, events and activities.

SET A SOCIAL CAP AND PLAN AHEAD
Withdraw some cash before going on a night out and leave your debit or credit cards at home – this is a superb remedy for overspending, although you should always ensure that you'll have the means to get home. If you know that you'll be out late or far from public transport, get the best possible taxi quote beforehand by using a comparison site.

FRIENDSHIP & MONEY: OIL & WATER.

- Mario Puzo

BE HONEST WITH FRIENDS

Many people are uncomfortable talking about money, particularly in big groups. There is an old episode of the seminal sitcom *Friends* that highlights this perfectly. Three of the less wealthy friends – Rachel, Joey and Phoebe – all become resentful towards their more well-off friends – Chandler, Ross and Monica – because they are asked to spend money on big birthday celebrations. The three 'poorer' friends then reluctantly bring the subject up at dinner with the 'richer' friends (after ordering cups of soup, side salads and a 'teeny' pizza to keep costs down) and everyone falls out.

You may be reluctant to tell your friends that an event is overpriced or that you're heading home early to save money. But you'll feel so much better if you clear the air. Talk about money. Make it clear that you're trying to stay within a budget. Always express gratitude for invitations but ask if adjustments/alternatives are possible. Your friends may have no idea that their suggestions are stretching your budget – they aren't mind readers.

TRY A GRACEFUL WHITE LIE

When all else fails, you can maintain relations (and financial equilibrium) with a little white lie.

- 'I have plans that day/night/weekend – have a wonderful time!'
- 'I'm attending another event that's been in the diary for weeks, but thanks for thinking of me.'
- 'I'd love to but I'd really like to focus on my work/family/partner/major hobby right now – but let's do something soon!'

Notice that I'm not saying words like: 'can't', 'shouldn't' or 'unable'. Those are words or phrases that imply I have no choice in the matter, that I'm being forced into turning opportunities down. If you're genuinely sorry that you can't make it or stay longer, say so, but once you convey that you're in charge of your time and money, not at the mercy of persuasion, others are more likely to respect your decisions.

Money in relationships

Female readers: hands up if you've been on a date and pulled out your purse at the end of an intimate meal, only to be greeted as if you had just produced an incendiary bomb.

Chaps seem to think that they have to be 'useful' to us girls in order to be attractive. The traditional role of men in generations gone by was to 'protect' and 'provide' – this behaviour is strongly

associated with masculinity in Western cultures. Of course, this isn't the case in all parts of the world. Did you know that women in the Aka tribe in Central Africa hunt and control distribution of resources? And what about the Indian state of Meghalaya, where women dominate land and property ownership and it is *men* who have to fight for equal rights?

The 'traditional' financial role of men is proving much less certain in a world where women's pay, opportunities and status keep getting better. So one easy way for the gents to show us that they can bring something to the table is to whip out the plastic and pay for everything on the table.

It's clear to see that our financial behaviour conveys all sorts of messages in the dating game – intentional or unintentional, desirable or undesirable. After all, how come it is taboo for a guy to bring coupons or vouchers to get money off a romantic meal? One girl's cheapskate could be another girl's frugal tactician.

And later down the line, who pays for what in a relationship can prove even more complex. Women can now vote, go to work, join the army, get their own mortgages, manage multinational corporations and run whole countries. So why can't they pay their way in relationships? Splitting bills and any costs incurred together is surely the fairest way, unless your partner earns substantially more than you or vice versa. In this case, perhaps you (or they) can contribute in proportion to salary. Let's say you earn twice as much as your partner – it may be fair to pay two-thirds of your rent or mortgage while your other half takes care of the rest.

If you still want a strong 'provider' component to your relationship, there are plenty of other ways to achieve this outside the financial realm. Some people think it's horribly sexist for a gentleman to open the door for his girl, put his jacket over her shoulder or carry her suitcase. Others think these are harmless acts of kindness that allow men to feel great. It's up to you to decide how to manage the dynamic of your relationship in a way that pleases both parties.

RESCUE ME: If you're single, set your saving goals, adjust your spending and insure yourself on the assumption that only *you* can take care of your needs, both now and in the future. Never operate in the belief that someone will come along and 'save' you. Otherwise, you're setting yourself up for a fall.

Money – the romance killer?

Relationships can be fraught with worries about money and what it signifies. Financial stuff shouldn't get in the way of having an amazing love life, yet this happens time and again.

Countless studies suggest that couples argue about money more than sex, children or anything else. And, according to research conducted by Kansas State University and Texas Tuch University, financial conflict is the single biggest predictor of divorce, regardless of income level.

So how can we avoid money causing relationship strife? By being open and frank about finances from the outset. Only then can you see eye to eye and figure out whether you're a good fit. Yes, that special someone may be on fire in the bedroom or a brilliant conversationalist. But do you know what they think about saving, spending and earning? Do they understand *your* financial values? These aren't sexy issues, I know, but they can make or break your relationship if things get serious.

We can go weeks, months, even years without bringing up money for fear that we'll spoil the romance. Then – bam! – we find ourselves in a committed relationship, making all sorts of plans for the future without knowing the first thing about our partner's approach to money. We only find out we're financially mismatched when it's too late. Before we know it, we're heading for the divorce courts, all for want of a proper conversation about this area earlier on.

DATING IS PRESSURE AND TENSION. WHAT IS A DATE, REALLY, BUT A JOB INTERVIEW THAT LASTS ALL NIGHT?

- Jerry Seinfeld

Obviously we shouldn't sit down and ask our date to produce their latest financial statements. And we don't *really* want to ask a prospective lover: 'So, thinking about buying property soon?' But perhaps some more upfront talking at an early stage might save misunderstanding and misery further down the line.

Financial heartbreak quiz

1 *Your newest date texts and suggests an expensive restaurant and concert tickets. You're not feeling particularly flush. You think:*

▶ *a.* The treat's on them.

▶ *b.* I must offer to pay my way, even though it's expensive.

▶ *c.* Perhaps we need to talk about splitting costs and finding cheaper things to do.

▶ *d.* I can't believe they expect me to spend all that money – I'm so annoyed.

2 *The bill arrives. You:*

▶ *a.* Offer to pay but back down immediately when your partner says 'I insist'.

▶ *b.* Have an argument about who pays.

▶ *c.* Reach a quick agreement to split the bill or pay in proportion to what you have consumed.

▶ *d.* Leave your wallet firmly in your bag. They should pay, no questions asked.

3 *The subject of money comes up. You:*

▶ *a.* Go quiet and change the subject quickly.

▶ *b.* Start asking detailed questions in the hope of finding out earnings, savings, etc.

▶ *c.* Welcome the opportunity to talk about this area.

▶ *d.* Get worked up about your combined financial problems before having a row.

If you answered mostly Cs, good job – you seem to have a positive approach to discussing money that will stand you in good stead. If you gravitated towards the other answers, you may be storing up problems for the future.

The four bases of dating

So you've just started dating someone. How quickly should you get to know them on a financial level?

FIRST BASE

Discuss your financial values and goals. Notice whether your partner is opening up or clamming up. Can you ascertain whether they've given much thought to their finances? Don't talk specifics: information about salary and savings should remain private at this stage, as you don't know the person well enough to trust them.

Suggested timeframe: Within the first four dates.

SECOND BASE

If your relationship progresses, find out more about your partner's underlying financial behaviour and beliefs. Always be honest about your situation so there is a decent quid pro quo going on. Do they have a 'live for today' ethos? Do they think about the future very much? Are they interested in home ownership, children, etc? Do they have debts, savings, investments? Do they pay off credit cards consistently or keep a budget?

There comes a point in every serious relationship where both partners deserve to know this information, so don't be ashamed about getting to the bottom of things. But reserve all judgements at this point. Just listen and take note.

Suggested timeframe: Within the first two to three months.

THIRD BASE

Your partner may not be 'there' in terms of sorting out their finances.

But don't rush to throw the towel in. There may be differences in how you both do things but take heart if your partner shows willing and is making small steps forward. Talk about ways that they can save more, spend less and clarify their long-term goals. Alarm bells should only start to ring if your partner is determined to stay the same and doesn't care about the consequences. Remember that you can never change a person's fundamental nature – it's better to face up to your partner's financial flaws now and honestly ask yourself if you can live with them.

Suggested timeframe: Ongoing. Discuss in the fullness of time.

FOURTH BASE

You may be on the cusp of some big joint decisions. These can include:

▸ Going on holiday together or buying tickets for a future event
▸ Moving in together, either by renting a place or buying
▸ Moving to a new city to support a partner
▸ Embarking on a long-distance relationship
▸ Buying a car together
▸ Getting engaged
▸ Getting married
▸ Dispensing with protection and trying for a baby
▸ Adopting a baby

At any of these points, you have to know whether your partner shares your financial goals or whether they have a very different idea of the future. If you're lucky, you may be pleasantly surprised to discover that you are completely in sync with your partner when it comes to money. The ideal scenario is one where both partners agree on all the big decisions – not just whether to get married, live together and have children, but where the family home should be and how to provide for/educate children.

Suggested timeframe: Before you make any long-term plans or commitments.

Before you commit ...

Even couples who are financially harmonious will be tested by costly expenses such as weddings, childcare and education. So here are some major areas to consider when deciding whether to tie up your future with someone else.

DEBT DRAMAS

Does your partner have a serious problem with debt? If so, there are two reasons to stop and think. Firstly, research has shown that people gradually adopt the same habits as their loved ones – for better or for worse. So your partner could start to subconsciously change your own financial behaviour, and not in a good way. Secondly, you may feel morally obliged to lend money or bail your partner out at various stages in the relationship. This will really take its toll on you, both financially and emotionally, and does nothing to solve the underlying problem. Paying off debts and doling out money merely puts off the inevitable and painful day of reckoning. Refusing to prop up your partner is, in fact, a kindness.

Many people are misguided in thinking they can 'rescue' someone in a long-term relationship. This is only possible if the person wants to be helped. If that individual won't get their act together, do what you need to do to protect yourself – even if it means calling it a day.

DIFFERENT DREAMS

Think very carefully before adjusting or abandoning any personal financial goals to be with someone. Have you sat down and discussed the potential trade-offs involved? How big are they? Do both parties feel happy about them, and do they cut both ways? Are both partners willing to reconsider them if they prove difficult to fulfil? If you don't have this conversation early on, bitterness could quickly bubble up.

BAD HABITS

Your partner may have some annoying financial peccadillos, but you need to pick your battles carefully. They may go over the top with gifts on special occasions, hoard money-saving coupons or be slow to give up a costly habit, but you probably have bugbears that require patience too. Sit down and discuss which habits are most likely to produce disagreement in your relationship.

Hopefully, you will shed light on the underlying emotions that drive those behaviours (or any violent reactions against them) so you can start to tackle them. For instance, financial arguments could be fuelled by fears about loss or reduction of income, which can be easily alleviated if you take out an income-protection policy or ramp up your savings.

Both of you should focus on small ways to tone down your more extreme behaviour. For instance, you may have a rule to do only homemade gifts on birthdays or spend coupons at the supermarket but not in restaurants on your date night. You may want to arrange regular chats with your partner to discuss coping strategies and monitor progress for giving up smoking and other expensive vices.

....

TIP ▶ *Couples can make some shrewd savings if they take charge of their finances. For instance, a couple that get married can reduce their tax bills by switching savings, investment or rental property into the name of the lower-earning spouse. Married couples can also reduce the tax bill incurred from the sale of certain assets, like shares and property, by transferring the gains into both partner's names. That is because each person has a capital gains tax allowance – that is, the amount we are allowed to gain from the sale of an asset without having to pay tax. So a couple can split those gains and house them within their individual allowances to reduce or even eliminate tax liability.*

**MARRIAGE IS
A SERIES OF
DESPERATE
ARGUMENTS
PEOPLE FEEL
PASSIONATELY
ABOUT.**

- Katherine Hepburn

Living with others

If you shack up with someone, it is worth keeping one eye on what might happen in the event of a split. You may recoil in horror at the idea of drawing up an agreement about what should happen if you split up. But a **prenuptial agreement** doesn't have to be a cold omen of a relationship breakdown. It can give you both peace of mind, boost communication about your finances and enhance mutual trust. Call it your love plan to take away the sting and take time over it to ensure it is fair to both parties. You would be well advised to enlist a solicitor to check it over. Your plan should also incorporate a will, which could protect you or your surviving partner should the very worst happen (particularly if you are unmarried).

Likewise, flatmates should also draw up a contingency plan just in case someone moves out abruptly. Will the departing individual see out the rest of their tenancy or will they find an immediate replacement? Will the person who leaves promise to keep paying the bills?

Before you buy a home with a partner or friend, pause and think. Do you have a plan in place if you decide to part ways? Would you sell up and split the money? Would one of you stay in the home and buy the other out? Perhaps you would get a lodger in to pay towards outstanding mortgage or rent payments. Knowing this puts your mind at rest and, in the worst-case scenario, provides every chance of personal solvency and good relations remaining intact.

CAUTION: It's worth remembering that when two people take out a joint mortgage, both are agreeing to be equally liable for the debt for the duration of the mortgage, not just while you live there. So both of you are responsible for ensuring the mortgage continues to be paid, and any failure to pay on time will damage both of your credit histories. You should also check you have enough life cover if you have a joint mortgage. Otherwise, one party could be left with a debt they cannot afford to pay off should the other pass away.

It is also a good idea to get your partner to draw up a budget as set out on page 79.

Once they have done this, you can compare their notes with yours and see where your expenses overlap. For essential bills, do you have an agreement about who pays what and how? At this point, it would also be very helpful to clarify ownership of your property (based on contributions towards the initial deposit and ongoing mortgage payments), cars and any other investments.

Secondly, have a good look at any debts your partner has incurred. You take partial responsibility for them if you sign a credit card agreement on their behalf. Also, are you paying part of someone's debt by sharing an account with them? This may be a very bad idea – if that person is overdrawn on your joint account, you share liability. In fact, your whole account could be emptied, leaving you at risk. It is best to keep your current accounts separate and agree to have the correct percentage paid by each partner for all essential bills via direct debit.

DEBTS PAID 'IN KIND'

Establish whether any debts in your household are paid 'in kind' and make sure all parties agree this is fair. What do I mean by this? Well, this was a very simple equation in, say, a 1950s household: the man went out to work and paid all the bills, and the woman looked after the children and ran the home. It is more complicated in modern households, where both partners may go out to work or multiple adult housemates are involved. So if one person in the home does most of the domestic duties/takes care of the children yet pays half of all bills, this could be a catalyst for a major row. An enlightened solution is to allow this person to pay a smaller share of household expenses, since they are giving up more of their time to keep the home running. Or perhaps there needs to be a more balanced division of duties. For instance, I live with my brother and we earn (roughly) the same amount. So I split the food bill with him. But since I do most of the shopping and cooking, he (theoretically) does a greater share of household cleaning and maintenance.

> # GETTING MONEY IS NOT ALL A MAN'S BUSINESS: TO CULTIVATE KINDNESS IS A VALUABLE PART OF THE BUSINESS OF LIFE.
>
> *– Samuel Johnson*

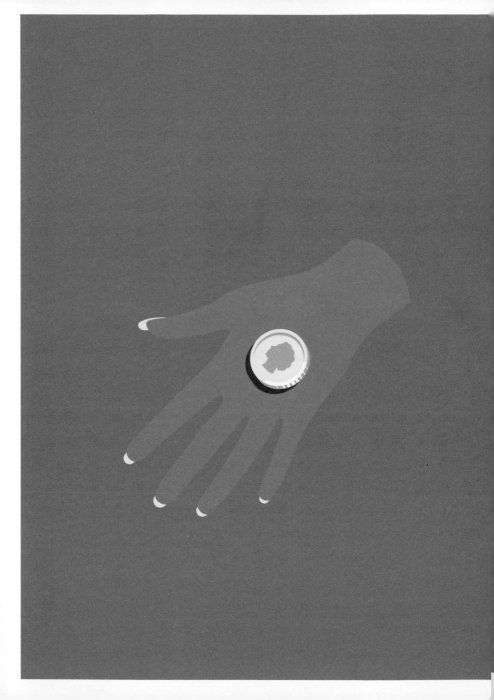

PART 7

DOING GOOD WITH YOUR MONEY

Money morals test

Take a look at the quiz below. Give yourself the following scores for each answer:

YES = 3 POINTS   MAYBE = 2 POINTS   NO = 1 POINT

1 I care about whether my clothes have been made in safe factories paying a decent wage.

2 It bothers me that my bank may be lending to dubious companies.

3 I would move my savings to an 'ethical' account if the rate was better.

4 It annoys me to think big internet corporations don't pay taxes in my country.

5 I would choose 'greener, cleaner' products if I could trust their advertising.

6 I would buy more locally produced food if it was available and competitive.

7 I would use small local shops if they were convenient and cheap enough.

8 I would change my energy supplier to one focused on renewables if it were made easy.

9 I would rather my pension wasn't being invested in payday lenders or mining firms evicting native peoples.

10 I would use my savings to support worthwhile businesses and projects if returns were better and it was 95 per cent safe.

11 I want any charity I support to be making the best use of its money.

12 I would rather buy a present from a shop supporting craftworkers in poor countries.

13 I would choose an 'ethical' product or savings account even if there was greater cost in doing so.

14 I would join a campaign to boycott powerful shopping websites who evade their responsibilities.

15 I would change my bank to one with a 'feel-good' promise even if it meant a bit of hassle.

16 I would buy from my local shop even if it was slightly more bother and expense.

17 I would be prepared to make Christmas gifts that helped people in poor countries.

18 I would give up a little of my time for a good cause rather than just make a donation.

YOUR SCORE:

49–54
You are already changing the world. Hurrah!

24–48
You would like to make some changes and feel better about how you use money.

18–23
You're not that bothered. But maybe I can get you to change your mind ...

A QUIET CONSCIENCE MAKES ONE STRONG!
– Anne Frank

Your shopping

In recent years there has been a significant rise in demand for organic produce, fair trade goods and more locally sourced food. Farmers' markets have sprung up, and supermarkets badgered into being more local-friendly.

Does your store of choice offer you plenty of produce from your region? Or are the shelves overflowing with goods that have travelled hundreds or thousands of 'food miles' to get there?

You might get real satisfaction in tweaking your shopping patterns so that your money goes straight into your local economy, helping it to get stronger and more balanced. Buying from local producers, smaller stores, markets, farmers' markets, charity events, mobile shops – it all boosts the feel-good factor in your spending.

GIVE WHEN YOU SPEND

Firstly, you can be more charitable by choosing shopping sites which donate commission from retailers to charity, such as Giving a Bit or Give as you Live. Retailers pay commission to these sites for directing people to their websites to make purchases. That commission can be donated to any charity of your choice and it is free to use.

There are also some shopping websites, including eBay, where you can also make a small donation to charity at the virtual checkout. And the charity-owned shopping website Care2Save gives 100 per cent of the money it makes through commission directly to the charity sector.

THOSE FASHION LABELS

You can extend this ethical spirit to your clothes shopping, by being aware of where items are made and whether workers are likely to have had a fair deal.

In recent years, many fashion retailers have been replicating the latest trends on the catwalk at knock-down prices. But that has only been achieved by using factories in countries with poor health and safety regulations. For instance, April 2013 saw the Rana Plaza factory in Bangladesh collapse, leaving 1,127 workers dead and another 2,000 injured.

According to the Ethical Trading Initiative, the Bangladesh Accord

has started improving conditions in the garment factories. But it still urges ethically minded consumers to check the country of origin on all clothing labels before buying.

Entrepreneur Jim McFarlane, who set up a cyclewear business in Scotland in 1992, has a strict policy when it comes to sourcing gloves and other items he cannot make in West Lothian. 'We don't touch Bangladesh or Pakistan, where there are endemic problems and policing is impossible,' he says. He uses fully vetted factories in China, and employs a native team to turn up unannounced on sites. 'We once had to wait nine months for gloves. I could have got them in 30 days in Pakistan, and at half the price, but we know how they do that, because they get kids to make them; in some cases it is bonded child labour.'

Jim says: 'It is good to be able to look customers in the eye and know what we say is true.'

Ethical Consumer magazine surveyed 25 clothes retailers in 2014 and gave top marks to Marks & Spencer, H&M and Zara, who were doing most to sell clothes made by properly paid and protected workers. The magazine also named the most ethical alternative clothing companies as People Tree, Living Crafts and THTC.

Australia is leading the way in encouraging shoppers to follow their conscience. The Australian app Shop Ethical! features the latest data from the Ethical Consumer Guide and is also based on information gathered from organisations including Greenpeace, Choose Cruelty Free, Reputex, Responsible Shopper and Friends of the Earth. It provides consumers with instant access to more than 2,800 products and related company information. *http://outware.com.au/shopethical*

THE GREENWASH BANDWAGON

Also, watch out for what's known as 'greenwashing' – this is when products or services are marketed to sound ethical, but really they aren't.

The Canadian government's Competition Bureau announced that more than 450,000 textile articles had been relabelled in its bid to prevent consumers being misled over 'green' claims for bamboo. It said so-called bamboo clothing was made from rayon fibres manufactured through a chemical process, and warned: 'Consumers may be paying a higher price ... on the assumption that the articles have environmentally friendly or health-enhancing qualities.' British consumers are also buying 'bamboo' products that are actually synthesised fibres which should really be called rayon or viscose.

Britain's Advertising Standards Authority receives hundreds of complaints a year about greenwashing. It has found that a machine boasting 'the greenest way to brew coffee' was no such thing and that palm oil is not 'the green answer'.

Palm oil is always worth a label check. Also known as sodium lareth sulphate, it pops up in everyday products such as soaps and detergents but its production is a major threat to the world's population of orangutans, as it destroys their habitat. According to Australia's Biome eco-stores, you can ditch palm oil and choose from a range of safer, healthier and eco-friendly alternatives.

What you are buying may sound green, but how far has it travelled to get to your store? That supposedly British wool may well have been sent to Australia and New Zealand to be cleaned and spun. Don't let them pull the wool over your eyes.

Your online habits

The search engine world is dominated by the likes of Google, but there are other options such as everyclick.com, where the website donates 50 per cent of its advertising revenue to charity. So far, it has raised millions.

Social media, meanwhile, is a powerful weapon in the hands of the disgruntled consumer. Companies are undoubtedly more attentive to bad vibes online these days. If you have been let down by a service or product, then go ahead: get it out there on social media. But send an e-mail or a letter too. You may just bag yourself a refund, free sample, voucher, gift card or even a free night's stay in the hotel where the fire alarm went off at 3 a.m – my parents did just that after an eventful trip and all it took was a forceful e-mail.

Your energy

Switching your energy supplier in the UK is now almost as easy as changing the picture on your desktop background. The energy market has a raft of suppliers offering lower prices than the big six established players, which is reason enough to take a look at them.

But did you know that firms like Good Energy offer energy from renewable sources only, yet still manage to undercut bigger rivals? Also, Ovo Energy pays interest on any credit that builds up in accounts through direct debit payments. This is in direct contrast to rivals who are happy to have hundreds of pounds of your unused money sitting there for months – for their benefit, not yours.

Your savings

What's all the fuss about crowdfunding? You may have heard about it working for big films, video games or even microbreweries. Technology has made it possible for individuals, worthy projects and new business ventures to cut out banks and raise cash directly from individuals via the internet. But is joining the crowd or entering the Dragons' Den the answer for your hard-earned savings? It might be.

There is a growing choice of platforms out there, but they all follow the basic rule of investing: the higher the return, the higher the risk. Lending to individuals or businesses will offer you returns that will almost certainly beat the bank. It is never as secure as depositing money with a bank, and may not be as accessible. But the best sites have sophisticated credit assessments and clever systems.

> **CAUTION:** All investment crowdfunding counts as a high-risk stake that you must be prepared to lose.

Your investments

If you want to earn a return on your money, but still feel warm and fuzzy inside, there's plenty you can do. Over the long term, statistics show that the performance of the average '**ethical fund**' compares favourably to the average conventional fund. An ethical fund is one that will not invest in sectors such as alcohol, tobacco and arms. However, not all funds are the same. Some will allow companies with only a small proportion of their business in such sectors, while others will seek out companies who behave best towards their workforce and the community. Everyone has their own preferences for ethical investing, so it's important to do some homework – for instance at YourEthicalMoney.org.

Surveys always find that a thumping majority of people with savings would like to see their money invested in socially or environmentally responsible businesses. Trouble is, they don't do much about it. The solution could be ethical funds. The question is – how do we know they're ethical?

Jason Hollands, managing director at brokers and advisers Tilney Bestinvest, says: 'The reality is that most businesses do not neatly fit into a black or white definition of good or bad. This means the largest holdings of most ethical funds are littered with well-recognised big companies, including banks, insurers, utilities and healthcare companies. That can leave those expecting to see their cash funnelled into social impact projects and renewable energy firms a little deflated.'

That is why many people wind up investing in exactly the kind of company they would knowingly avoid. Even the church isn't immune to such mistakes. In 2013, the Church of England discovered it had £75,000 of investments indirectly backing payday lender Wonga, against which the Archbishop of Canterbury had campaigned!

That's because most UK 'ethical' funds do not fully disclose what they invest in. Many funds use outdated 'tick box' models, with 63 per cent of funds rejecting stocks linked to alcohol but only 11 per cent checking for possible connections with child labour, according to the ShareAction group in 2014. It said most fund groups simply want an 'ethical badge' on a fund.

The sectors that ethical investment funds typically avoid or negatively screen are :

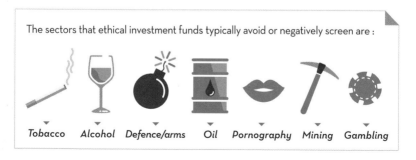

Tobacco   Alcohol   Defence/arms   Oil   Pornography   Mining   Gambling

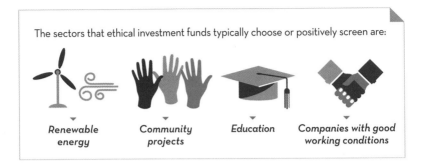

The sectors that ethical investment funds typically choose or positively screen are:

Renewable energy   *Community projects*   *Education*   *Companies with good working conditions*

So who offers the real deal? ShareAction has awarded high marks to F&C Investments, which launched the UK market's first ethical fund in 1984, and to Standard Life, WHEB, The Co-operative and Jupiter, followed by Rathbones, Ecclesiastical and Alliance Trust.

A new development in the UK market in 2014 was charity bonds. The first one offered investors a 4.4 per cent return over seven years, and had to close early after raising £11 million in a couple of weeks. It was issued by Golden Lane, the housing arm of learning disability charity Mencap, to fund the building of 30 quality homes for 100 people with a learning disability.

Retail charity bonds can be held in UK Individual Savings Accounts and self-invested personal pensions, and the bonds may have terms of five to ten years, with fixed returns of 4-5 per cent. This is part of a more principled outlook in investment. The Threadneedle Social Bond Fund, for instance, invests in bonds issued by charities, social enterprises and businesses delivering positive impact in specific areas.

CAUTION: Unlike most crowdfunding loans, where your cash is spread across lots of individual borrowers, a bond means one organisation has to pay you back. So there is no guarantee it will happen, and no protection from the Financial Services Compensation Scheme.

Your banking

When it comes to banking and saving, it's all about doing your homework.

The Co-operative Bank is upfront about its ethical lending policies – but its savings rates are underwhelming. Dutch bank Triodos lends only to sustainable, locally positive projects *and* pays competitive savings rates.

Credit unions are another great way to save and borrow with discipline, with the bonus that you're contributing to an organisation working only for its members.

Your giving

Everyone gives to charity, but do you have a plan for when you say yes, and when it's: 'sorry, no?'

Here are some common charitable inducements that crop up in everyday life:
▶ Workplace e-mails asking you to sponsor marathons, cycle treks and mountain climbing.
▶ Charity fundraisers in the street (known to many irritated pedestrians as 'chuggers'/'charity muggers').
▶ Door-to-door fundraisers.

Giving to every cause that tugs at your heartstrings is admirable but perhaps not sustainable. However, it is equally unwise to hoard all your money for yourself. It has been proved by countless studies that giving money and time to others is the quickest route to long-term contentment. So you have to decide what kind of giving works for you.

It may be worth sticking to a strict policy; decide when and where you will give money to charity, and what will be your limit. Also decide when to politely decline and why – be it down to principle or sheer lack of cash to go around.

AUDIT YOUR GIVING

If you think you ought to give more, or less, or do it better, you may as well start by monitoring your charitable donations. Do you know how much money you're parting with – and why?

GOOD CAUSE	NEVER	SOMETIMES	ALWAYS	£ PER MONTH
Regular donations	☐ (tick)	☐	☐	
Work sponsoring	☐	☐	☐	
Family sponsoring	☐	☐	☐	
TV appeals	☐	☐	☐	
Postal appeals	☐	☐	☐	
Emergency appeals	☐	☐	☐	
Sign up on street	☐	☐	☐	
Box on street	☐	☐	☐	
Collection at door	☐	☐	☐	
Homeless people	☐	☐	☐	
Buskers	☐	☐	☐	

Whatever the total is, reflect on whether you are happy with this quantity of giving. Also consider whether you could volunteer or offer your skills, talents or time for certain charitable causes instead.

Your special occasions

Special occasions can be a common trigger for spending money – not least because retailers like us to do so! Whether it's Mothering Sunday, Father's Day or Valentine's, do you feel a compulsion to buy something to please your loved ones?

Perhaps you have set an expectation in your family that you will always buy lavish gifts or tokens of appreciation on these dates. It can be a pressurising ritual but you can always break out of it – indeed, why not think of other, more personal ways to show your love?

CHRISTMAS

Christmas can be one of the biggest causes of overspending. According to a survey by overseas development charity CARE International, people in the UK reckon they waste an average of nearly £50 each on Christmas presents that are not really wanted. Another survey, by Scottish development charity SCIAF, found that twice as many people would rather have a 'real gift' made on their behalf for a family in a third-world village than receive a pair of socks.

There are a number of 'real gifts' schemes available; a typical UK scheme asks you to spend £26 to send a child to school, which pays for notebooks, pens and uniforms, or £40 towards 'safe water for five families', which pays for wells and other water projects. The money raised from these gifts helps people in Africa, Asia and Latin America, and other giving options include seeds, chickens, pigs and medicines.

Then there is Lendwithcare, an innovative scheme that enables people living in the UK to offer small loans to entrepreneurs running their own businesses in poor communities around the world. It has already lent more than £5 million to about 4,000 entrepreneurs.

CARE International, which runs the scheme, says: 'It may be a farmer in Cambodia who is seeking a loan to buy seeds, or a shopkeeper in Togo looking for funds to buy new supplies – enabling them to trade their own way out of poverty.'

But if you would rather that charity begins at home, you might want to think about whether your intended good cause is also good at managing funds effectively. Big, complex charities handling large budgets often pay large salaries to their top people, which can be controversial. If this bothers you, there are other models – the Salvation Army springs to mind. Organisations such as New Philanthropy Capital (www.thinknpc.org) analyse charities and report on how effective they are.

Just remember – charity doesn't have to be a chore or a bore. Give it some meaning and reflect on how to do more good with your money. Making ethical finance a part of your everyday life is a decision you won't regret.

TO BE DOING GOOD DEEDS IS MAN'S MOST GLORIOUS TASK.

– *Sophocles*

THE ECONOMICS OF HAPPINESS

Rising incomes = rising happiness?

Finally, take comfort from recent research showing that economic progress may not add very much to our enjoyment of life. The new field of 'happiness economics' suggests that going beyond a certain level of prosperity, both as a country and as an individual, means very little. Our satisfaction with life peaks when incomes per head reach £22,000 a year.

Eugenio Proto of Warwick University, who conducted the research alongside Aldo Rustichini of University of Minnesota, said: 'Our new analysis has one very surprising finding which has not been reported before – that life satisfaction appears to dip beyond a certain level of wealth. In our study we see evidence that this is down to changes in the aspiration levels of people living in the richest countries.'

The research found a strong link between rising incomes and happiness in poor countries – but only up to a point. People in poorer nations, those with average incomes below £4,100 per person, were 12 per cent less likely to report the highest level of life satisfaction than those in the slightly better-off countries (where average incomes are about £11,000). But in countries with average incomes above £12,000 per person, the gap was much smaller between their citizens' reported happiness and that seen in the richest countries (where average incomes are £33,000). Even more interesting is that once nations have an average wealth of £22,000 per person, the happiness rating peaks and then starts to fall.

That last statistic helps to prove one of the most important money truths of all: happiness starts to fall away as individuals stop appreciating what they have, and start chasing after what they don't.

So there you go. It's been scientifically proven that money – beyond a certain level – will not make you happy. In fact, hunting those highly paid careers (or partners!) and pining for luxury is making many of us miserable.

But that doesn't mean that we should disregard the role of money in our lives - far from it. Whether we're earning, spending, saving or giving it away, money is a major fact of life. We have no choice but to deal with it every day, every week, every month. What we can choose is *how* we deal with it. It can be managed or squandered, grown or neglected, put in its place or allowed to dominate everything. It can be emotionally toxic or highly empowering. It can be a force for good or for bad. It's totally up to you. But just remember: things don't have to carry on as they were. We can decide to do things differently. We all have change to spare ...

A WISE MAN SHOULD HAVE MONEY IN HIS HEAD, BUT NOT IN HIS HEART.

- Jonathon Swift

THANK
YOUS

I want to thank the team at Hardie Grant for allowing me to write this book in my own way. I am particularly grateful to Kate Pollard, who has been wonderfully supportive and made the whole process a total pleasure. Special thanks also go to Louise Francis, who has done a huge amount to make this book as accurate and coherent as possible, and the ever-helpful Kajal Mistry. I also want to thank Julia Murray for the fabulous illustrations and design that have really brought this book alive.

I am also grateful to Stuart Carmichael from the Debt Support

Trust for his contribution and Kim Stephenson, whose work on financial psychology has been very helpful. Extra thanks go to the late Jane Furnival and Alvin Hall, the Open University, Baroness Altmann and Walter Mischel whose approaches to personal finance have inspired me the most whilst researching this book.

Finally, words can't really express the gratitude I feel towards my brother, Matt, and my parents, Norma and Simon, who have been the rock of my life and helped me in countless ways. None of this would have been possible without my magnificent family.

ABOUT THE
AUTHOR

Born and brought up in Edinburgh, Iona Bain was working as a freelance musician and journalist when the UK recession hit her generation hard. Aged 23 (and with an Oxford music degree) she decided to start a blog about young people and money to provide solidarity for all those struggling with their finances. Youngmoneyblog.co.uk quickly became a must-visit site for all those trying to get to grips with personal finance at an early stage. This led to Iona fronting a BBC education campaign in 2013, which involved a documentary, webcast and special edition of the Radio 1 Sunday Surgery.

As well as running the blog, Iona is now personal finance correspondent at the *Herald* newspaper and has written for the *Daily Mail, Daily Mirror, Independent* and *The Sunday Times,* among other titles. She has appeared on Channel 4 News and the Max Keiser Report and regularly speaks at events. Iona has also recently become a tech entrepreneur thanks to her involvement with FeeForAll, a consumer website in the property sector. She still loves playing music and her songs can be heard at soundcloud.com/ionabain.

Spare Change by Iona Bain

First published in 2016 by Hardie Grant Books

Hardie Grant Books (UK)
5th & 6th Floors
52–54 Southwark Street
London SE1 1UN
www.hardiegrant.co.uk

Hardie Grant Books (Australia)
Ground Floor, Building 1
658 Church Street
Melbourne, VIC 3121
www.hardiegrant.com.au

British Library Cataloguing-in-Publication Data. A catalogue
record for this book is available from the British Library.

ISBN: 978-1-78488-023-1

Publisher: Kate Pollard
Senior Editor: Kajal Mistry
Internal and Cover Design: Julia Murray
Internal and Cover Illustrations: Julia Murray
Editorial Assistant: Hannah Roberts
Copy Editor: Louise Francis
Proofreader: Nicky Jeans
Indexer: Cathy Heath
Colour Reproduction by p2d

Printed and bound in China by 1010

10 9 8 7 6 5 4 3 2 1

IONA BAIN

SPARE CHANGE

IONA BAIN

SPARE CHANGE

BETTER WAYS TO MANAGE MONEY

hardie grant books